GOVERNMENT PROCEDURES AND OPERATIONS

FEDERAL CROP INSURANCE

FARM BILL PROVISIONS, TRENDS, AND PREMIUM REDUCTION CONSIDERATIONS

GOVERNMENT PROCEDURES AND OPERATIONS

Additional books in this series can be found on Nova's website under the Series tab.

Additional e-books in this series can be found on Nova's website under the e-book tab.

GOVERNMENT PROCEDURES AND OPERATIONS

FEDERAL CROP INSURANCE

FARM BILL PROVISIONS, TRENDS, AND PREMIUM REDUCTION CONSIDERATIONS

TRISTAN E. BONNER
EDITOR

nova publishers
New York

For permission to use material from this book please contact us:
Telephone 631-231-7269; Fax 631-231-8175
Web Site: http://www.novapublishers.com

Library of Congress Cataloging-in-Publication Data

ISBN: 978-1-63463-688-9

Published by Nova Science Publishers, Inc. † New York

CONTENTS

PREFACE

This book provides a primer on the federal crop insurance program and briefly summarizes changes to the program by the 2014 farm bill.

Chapter 1 – The federal crop insurance program began in 1938 when Congress authorized the Federal Crop Insurance Corporation. The current program, which is administered by the U.S. Department of Agriculture's Risk Management Agency (RMA), provides producers with risk management tools to address crop yield and/or revenue losses for about 130 crops. The federal farm safety net also includes the farm commodity support programs, which provide price and income support for a much narrower list of "covered and loan commodities" such as corn, wheat, rice, and peanuts.

In purchasing a crop insurance policy, a producer growing an insurable crop selects a level of coverage and pays a portion of the premium—or none of it in the case of catastrophic coverage— which increases as the level of coverage rises. The federal government pays the rest of the premium (62%, on average, in 2013). Insurance policies are sold and completely serviced through 18 approved private insurance companies. As spelled out in a Standard Reinsurance Agreement (SRA), the insurance companies' losses are reinsured by USDA, and their administrative and operating costs are reimbursed by the federal government (i.e., not farmers).

In 2013, federal crop insurance policies covered 296 million acres. Major crops are covered in most counties where they are grown. Four crops—corn, cotton, soybeans, and wheat—accounted for more than 70% of total acres enrolled in crop insurance. Most crop insurance policies are either yield-based or revenue-based. For yield-based policies, a producer can receive an indemnity if there is a yield loss relative to the farmer's "normal" (historical) yield. Revenue-based policies protect against crop revenue loss resulting from declines in yield, price, or both. Other insurance products protect against losses in whole farm revenue (rather than just for an individual crop) or gross margins for livestock enterprises.

Chapter 2 – The enacted 2014 farm bill (the Agricultural Act of 2014; P.L. 113-79) enhances the federal crop insurance program by expanding its scope, covering a greater share of farm losses, and making other modifications that broaden policy coverage. The changes stem from the desire of many in Congress, particularly members of the agriculture committees, to bolster what they consider to be the most significant aspect of the farm safety net.

Under the federal crop insurance program, which is administered by the U.S. Department of Agriculture's Risk Management Agency (RMA), producers purchase subsidized policies to help manage financial risks associated with crop yield or revenue losses, primarily from natural disasters. In contrast, farm commodity programs apply to a narrower set of "program" crops, require no participation fees, and make payments when prices fall below statutory minimums or when crop revenue is low relative to historical levels.

A prominent crop insurance feature of the 2014 farm bill is the authorization of policies designed to reimburse "shallow losses"—an insured producer's out-of-pocket loss associated with the policy deductible. A new crop insurance policy called Stacked Income Protection Plan (STAX) is made available for upland cotton producers, while the Supplemental Coverage Option (SCO) is made available for other crops. The STAX policy indemnifies losses in county revenue of greater than 10% of expected revenue but not more than the deductible level (e.g., 25%) selected by the producer for the underlying individual policy. (It can also be purchased as a stand-alone policy.) Similarly, SCO is based on expected county revenue (or yields) and covers part of the deductible under the producer's underlying policy. The government subsidy as a share of the policy premium is set at 80% for STAX and 65% for SCO.

A variety of additional provisions are expected to expand existing crop insurance products or require examination of the potential for new products, including those that would benefit specialty crops and animal agriculture. Provisions revise the value of crop insurance for organic crops to reflect generally higher prices of organic (not conventional) crops. USDA is also required to conduct more research on whole farm revenue insurance with higher coverage levels than currently available. Studies or policies are also required for insuring (1) specialty crop producers for food safety and contamination-related losses, (2) swine producers for a catastrophic disease event, (3) producers of catfish against reduction in the margin between the market prices and production costs, (4) commercial poultry production against business disruptions caused by integrator bankruptcy, (5) poultry producers for a catastrophic event, (6) producers of biomass sorghum or sweet sorghum grown as feedstock for renewable energy, and (7) alfalfa producers. A peanut revenue insurance product and rice margin insurance also are mandated. Another provision provides funding for index weather insurance for protecting against weather.

To address conservation concerns, the 2014 farm bill links eligibility for crop insurance premium subsidies to compliance with wetland and conservation requirements for highly erodible land. Also, crop insurance subsidies are reduced for plantings on native sod acreage in certain states.

In total, the crop insurance title increases funding for crop insurance by an additional \$5.7 billion over 10 years relative to projected levels that assumed no change in policy. The largest cost items are for STAX (\$3.3 billion) and SCO (\$1.7 billion), according to the Congressional Budget Office. A controversial item not included in P.L. 113-79 was the reduction of premium subsidies for high-income farmers, which had been included in the Senate farm bill but not the House bill.

Chapter 3 – Federally subsidized crop insurance, which farmers can buy to help manage the risk inherent in farming, has become one of the most important programs in the farm safety net. Revenue policies, which protect farmers against crop revenue loss from declines in production or price, are the most popular policy type and account for nearly 80 percent of all premium subsidies. The crop insurance program's cost has come under scrutiny while the nation's budgetary pressures have been increasing.

GAO was asked to look at the cost of the crop insurance program. This report examines (1) trends in federal crop insurance costs and farm sector income and wealth from 2003 through 2012 and (2) the potential savings to the government and impacts on farmers, if any, of reducing federal premium subsidies for revenue policies. GAO analyzed USDA crop insurance program data and farm sector income and wealth data from 2003 through 2012 (most recent year with complete crop insurance data); reviewed economic literature and documents from stakeholders including farm industry groups and researchers; and interviewed USDA officials.

In: Federal Crop Insurance
Editor: Tristan E. Bonner
ISBN: 978-1-63463-688-9

Chapter 1

FEDERAL CROP INSURANCE: BACKGROUND*

Dennis A. Shields

SUMMARY

The federal crop insurance program began in 1938 when Congress authorized the Federal Crop Insurance Corporation. The current program, which is administered by the U.S. Department of Agriculture's Risk Management Agency (RMA), provides producers with risk management tools to address crop yield and/or revenue losses for about 130 crops. The federal farm safety net also includes the farm commodity support programs, which provide price and income support for a much narrower list of "covered and loan commodities" such as corn, wheat, rice, and peanuts.

In purchasing a crop insurance policy, a producer growing an insurable crop selects a level of coverage and pays a portion of the premium—or none of it in the case of catastrophic coverage— which increases as the level of coverage rises. The federal government pays the rest of the premium (62%, on average, in 2013). Insurance policies are sold and completely serviced through 18 approved private insurance companies. As spelled out in a Standard Reinsurance Agreement (SRA), the insurance companies' losses are reinsured by USDA, and their administrative and operating costs are reimbursed by the federal government (i.e., not farmers).

* This is an edited, reformatted and augmented version of a Congressional Research Service publication R40532, prepared for Members and Committees of Congress, dated June 3, 2014.

In 2013, federal crop insurance policies covered 296 million acres. Major crops are covered in most counties where they are grown. Four crops—corn, cotton, soybeans, and wheat—accounted for more than 70% of total acres enrolled in crop insurance. Most crop insurance policies are either yield-based or revenue-based. For yield-based policies, a producer can receive an indemnity if there is a yield loss relative to the farmer's "normal" (historical) yield. Revenue-based policies protect against crop revenue loss resulting from declines in yield, price, or both. Other insurance products protect against losses in whole farm revenue (rather than just for an individual crop) or gross margins for livestock enterprises.

Government costs for crop insurance have increased substantially in recent years. After ranging between $2.1 billion and $3.9 billion during FY2000-FY2007, costs rose to $7 billion in FY2009 as higher policy premiums from rising crop prices drove up premium subsidies to farmers and expense reimbursements (which are based on total premiums) to private insurance companies. Costs rose further to $11.3 billion in FY2011 and $14.1 billion in FY2012 when crop prices surged again and poor weather resulted in program losses. In FY2013, total program costs declined to $6.0 billion with a return to more favorable weather and smaller crop losses.

Federal outlays for crop insurance exceed those for the farm commodity support programs, making crop insurance the most significant cost component of the farm safety net and a potential target for deficit reduction. Insurance companies, farm groups, and some Members of Congress are concerned that reductions in federal support could negatively impact the financial health of the industry and possibly jeopardize the delivery of crop insurance to farmers. A main goal is saving federal dollars without adversely affecting farmer participation, policy coverage, or industry interest in selling and servicing insurance products to farmers. From a farm policy standpoint, policy makers and observers alike remain concerned about how the crop insurance program interacts with farm commodity programs and whether together they provide a means for helping farmers deal with business risk at a cost that is acceptable to taxpayers.

In the 2014 farm bill (P.L. 113-79), Congress expanded the federal crop insurance program by authorizing additional policies for farmers and requiring examination of potential products, including those that would benefit specialty crops and animal agriculture. As background to a report summarizing farm bill changes (CRS Report *Crop Insurance Provisions in the 2014 Farm Bill (P.L. 113-79)*, this report explains the basic components of the crop insurance program, its operation, and federal costs.

For many farmers, federal crop insurance is the most important component of the farm safety net, given the breadth of commodity coverage, from apples to wheat, and the capability to reimburse producers for crop losses. The federal crop insurance program makes available subsidized policies to help farmers manage risk associated with natural disasters, including drought, excess moisture, and other perils. The average annual federal cost is approximately $8 billion.

This report provides a primer on the federal crop insurance program and briefly summarizes changes to the program by the 2014 farm bill (P.L. 113-79).

The farm safety net also includes the farm commodity support programs, which provide price and income support for a much narrower list of "covered and loan commodities" such as corn, soybeans, wheat, rice, and peanuts. Agricultural disaster programs are available for producers owning livestock or fruit trees.

CROP INSURANCE HISTORY

Farming is generally regarded as a financially risky enterprise. Most agricultural production is subject to the vagaries of weather, and shifts in agricultural supply and demand often result in volatile market prices. Farm financial risk, periods of low returns, and the importance of agriculture in the nation's economy during the early to mid-1900s led to the development of federal policies that financially supported farmers, primarily through commodity price mechanisms. Today's farm commodity policies—authorized in the 2008 farm bill—have their roots in the 1930s.

During the same era, Congress also first authorized federal crop insurance as an experiment to address the effects of the Great Depression and crop losses seen in the Dust Bowl. In 1938, the Federal Crop Insurance Corporation (FCIC) was created to carry out the program, which focused on major crops in major producing regions. The availability of federal crop insurance remained limited until passage of the Federal Crop Insurance Act of 1980 (P.L. 96-365), which expanded crop insurance to many more crops and regions of the country. Congress enhanced the crop insurance program, including greater subsidy levels, in 1994 and again in 2000 in order to encourage greater participation. The changes also expanded the role of the private sector in developing new products that would help farmers manage their risks.[1] Today, many banks, when making operating loans, require that farmers purchase crop insurance.

The federal crop insurance program is permanently authorized by the Federal Crop Insurance Act, as amended (7 U.S.C. 1501 et seq.). It is periodically modified. For example, Congress chose to revise the legislation in the 2008 farm bill (P.L. 110-246) to achieve budget savings and to supplement crop insurance with a permanent disaster payment program. The 2014 farm bill (P.L. 113-79) expanded the program and increased budget outlays.[2] The U.S. Department of Agriculture's (USDA's) Risk Management Agency (RMA) operates and manages the FCIC.

PROGRAM BASICS

The federal crop insurance program provides producers with risk management tools to address crop yield and/or revenue losses on farms. Guarantees are established just prior to planting, based on historical yields and expected market prices (not statutory prices used in farm programs). Insurance policies are sold and completely serviced through 18 approved private insurance companies. Independent insurance agents are paid sales commissions by the companies. The insurance companies' losses are reinsured by USDA, and their administrative and operating costs are reimbursed by the federal government (see *Figure 1* and "Federal Program Costs," below).

In purchasing a policy, a producer growing an insurable crop selects a level of coverage and pays a portion of the premium, which increases as the level of coverage rises. The remainder of the premium is covered by the federal government (about 62% of total premium, on average, is paid by the government).[3] In the case of catastrophic coverage, the government pays the full premium. Also, the government, not the farmer, pays for the cost of selling and servicing all policies. In the absence of premium subsidies and free delivery, farmer participation in the crop insurance program and/or purchased coverage levels would be lower. A major benefit for producers is the timely payment for crop losses (about 30 days after the farmer signs the claim form).

In 2013, crop insurance policies covered 296 million acres (*Figure 2*). Approximately 83% of U.S. crop acreage is insured under the federal crop insurance program. Major crops are insurable in most counties where they are grown.[4] Four crops—corn, cotton, soybeans, and wheat— accounted for more than 70% of total enrolled acres. For these major crops, a large share of plantings is covered by crop insurance: corn at 84% of plantings; cotton, 94%; soybeans, 84%; and wheat, 83%.

Policies for less widely produced crops are available in primary growing areas. Examples include dry peas, blueberries, citrus, pumpkins, and walnuts. In total, policies are available for about 130 crops (including coverage on a variety of fruit trees, nursery crops, pasture, rangeland, and forage).[5]

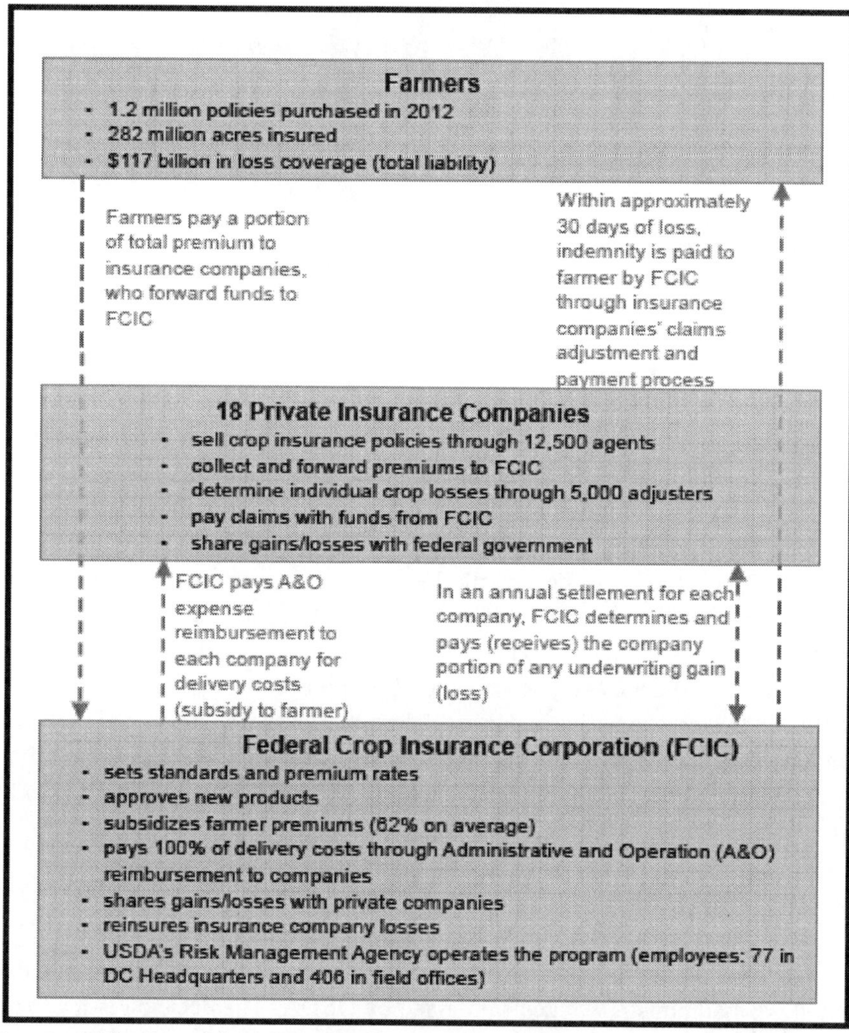

Source: CRS, adapted from U.S. Department of Agriculture and industry sources.

Figure 1. Federal Crop Insurance Program.

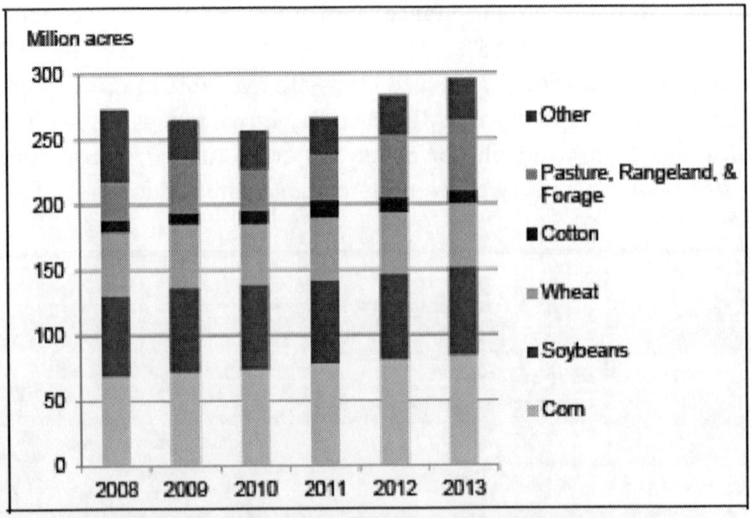

Source: U.S. Department of Agriculture, Risk Management Agency.

Figure 2. Insured Acres by Crop Year.

Many specialty crop producers depend on crop insurance as the only "safety net" for their operation, unlike field crop producers, who are also eligible for farm commodity program payments.[6] In the specialty crop category, insured acreage as a share of total acreage is 73% for fruits and nuts and 32% for vegetables.[7]

Crop insurance is not necessarily limited to crops. Relatively new or pilot programs protect livestock and dairy producers from loss of gross margin or price declines.[8] Livestock producers can also insure against hay and forage losses through the Pasture, Rangeland, and Forage program, which uses a rainfall index or vegetative index to determine loss.[9] In 2013, USDA/RMA announced a pilot program for crop year 2014 that covers annual hay production in North Dakota, South Dakota, Nebraska, Oklahoma, and Texas.[10]

Policy Availability

The availability of crop insurance for a particular crop in a particular region is an administrative decision made by USDA. The decision is made on a crop-by-crop and county-by-county basis, based on farmer demand for coverage and the level of risk associated with the crop in the region, among other factors. Developing new products can be costly, and a significant challenge is obtaining credible data (yield and price) to create an actuarially sound product. The process usually starts with a pilot program, which is conducted for about three years in order for RMA to gain experience and test the program components before it becomes more widely available. Alternatively, a policy can be reviewed and later discontinued if it fails to perform at an acceptable level (e.g., low participation or high losses).

Some policies remain as a pilot for years. For example, the forage (alfalfa) seed insurance policy was introduced in 2002 as a pilot program to provide insurance coverage to alfalfa seed farmers. On May 29, 2014, USDA announced that it would be converted to a permanent policy for the 2015 crop year. During the pilot period, USDA determined an insurance need for hybrid production and made a program change to provide coverage for growers contracting for production of hybrid alfalfa seed.

Regions without Coverage

In regions where a policy is not available, farmers may request from the appropriate regional office that RMA expand the program to their county.[11] A producer also may request insurance coverage under a written agreement, which is a document designed to provide crop insurance for insurable crops when coverage or rates are unavailable.[12]

When crop insurance is not available, USDA's noninsured crop disaster assistance program (NAP) provides the equivalent of catastrophic coverage (for yield losses greater than 50%) if purchased by the producer. Additional coverage (for yield losses greater than 35%) has been made available by the 2014 farm bill. To be eligible for a NAP payment, a producer first must apply for coverage under the program by the application closing date, which varies by crop, but is generally about 30 days prior to the final planting date for an annual crop. As with catastrophic crop insurance, NAP applicants pay an administrative fee (currently $250 per crop). No premiums are required.[13]

Enhancing Existing Coverage

RMA also regularly responds to requests from commodity organizations or industry representatives for enhancements to existing coverage, such as adding revenue coverage and organic practice coverage or trend yield adjustments to better reflect a producer's liability. In some cases, RMA has not pursued policies for particular commodities because producers have expressed concerns that offering insurance could adversely affect the market (i.e., because an insurance policy reduces producer risk, farmers may plant more acreage, which could drive down prices and total crop revenue). This has been a concern for many vegetable crops and explains in part lower levels of insured vegetable acreage compared with other crops.[14]

Actuarial Soundness

Current law requires that RMA strive for actuarial soundness for the entire federal crop insurance program (that is, indemnities should equal total premiums, including premium subsidies).[15] As a result, RMA must set premium rates to only cover expected losses and a reasonable reserve. The agency is also required to conduct periodic reviews of its rate-setting methodology, which sets premium rates according to the average historical rate of loss (e.g., if policies pay out 10% of their value, on average, then the rate should be 10%). Based on a review completed in July 2011, RMA adjusted its methodology for several major commodities to give more weight to recent years and to make other changes.[16]

Types of Insurance

Federal crop insurance policies are generally either yield-based or revenue-based. For most yield-based policies, a producer can receive an indemnity if there is a yield loss relative to the farmer's "normal" (historical) yield. Revenue-based policies were developed after yield-based policies, in the mid-1990s, to protect against crop revenue loss resulting from declines during the growing season in yield, price, or both. The most recent addition has been products that protect against losses in whole farm revenue rather than just for an individual crop. For both yield- and revenue-based policies, the price used to set the guarantee is based only on the expected price for the upcoming season, and is reset every year. This is in contrast to farm programs which either have price guarantees set in statute or use historical average prices and are designed to protect against longer-term price declines.

These two basic forms—yield-based and revenue-based—are discussed below, followed by a brief explanation of whole farm insurance. The text boxes in this report entitled "Crop Insurance Examples: Yield-Based vs. Revenue-Based" and "Federal Crop Insurance: Range of Coverage and Policies" explain program operation within the two broad categories.

Slightly more than 1.2 million crop insurance policies were active in 2013, with revenue-based policies accounting for three-quarters of the total (*Figure*

3), and the remainder being yield-based policies. On a premium basis, revenue policies account for 84% of all policies.

Yield-Based Insurance

When purchasing a crop insurance policy, a producer is assigned (1) a "normal" crop yield based on the producer's actual production history, and (2) a price for his commodity based on estimated market conditions. The producer can then select a percentage of his normal yield to be insured and a percentage of the price he wishes to receive when crop losses exceed the selected loss threshold. The level of crop yield coverage is viewed by farmers as a critical feature of crop insurance, and a major determinant of whether a farmer will purchase insurance.[17]

(policies earning premiums in 2013 = 1.22 million)

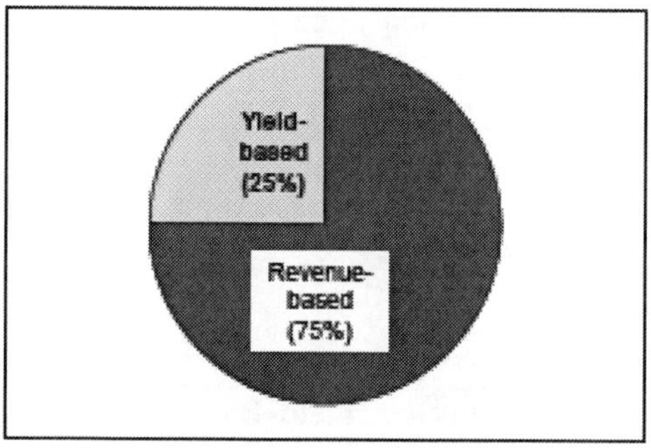

Source: U.S. Department of Agriculture, Risk Management Agency.

Notes: When calculated by share of premiums paid, yield-based policies account for 16% of total policies and revenue-based policies account for 84%. Index and "dollar" policies are included in yield-based total.

Figure 3. Types of Crop Insurance Policies.

In determining what a normal production level is for an insurable farmer, USDA requires the producer to present actual annual crop yields (usually stated on a bushel-per-acre basis) for the last 4 to 10 years. The simple average of a producer's annual crop yield over this time period then serves as the producer's actual production history (APH). If a farmer does not have adequate records, he can be assigned a transition yield (T-yield) for each missing year of data, which is based on average county yields for the crop.

The most basic policy is called catastrophic (CAT) coverage. The premium for this level of coverage is completely subsidized by the federal government. The farmer pays an administrative fee for CAT coverage ($300 per crop per county), and in return can receive a payment on losses in excess of 50% of normal yield, equal to 55% of the estimated market price of the crop (called 50/55 coverage).

Coverage levels that are higher than CAT are called "buy-up" coverage, and most farmer purchase buy-up policies because of the additional protection.[18] For an additional premium paid by the producer, and partially subsidized by the government (see "Crop Insurance Premium Subsidies," below), a producer can "buy up" the 50/55 catastrophic coverage to any equivalent level of coverage between 50/100 and 75/100 (i.e., up to 75% of "normal" crop yield and 100% of the estimated market price). In limited areas, production can be insured up to the 85/100 level of coverage.

The policy name depends on how pricing is determined for the crop. "APH" policies use a projected price determined by RMA, while "Yield Protection" policies use a projected price based on the commodity exchange markets. For example, polices are APH for plums and Yield Protection for wheat. Several other policies, including Area Yield Protection (formerly called Group Risk Plan) and Dollar Plan (see box), are not widely used but can be important for certain crops. Some of these policies use an area-wide index—such as county-level yield in the case of the Area Yield Protection—to measure losses.

Crop Insurance Examples: Yield-Based vs. Revenue-Based

Two basic forms of crop insurance are yield-based and revenue-based. Yield-based insurance provides an indemnity when the actual yield falls below the guarantee level. Revenue-based insurance provides an indemnity when the revenue (actual yield x price) falls below the guarantee.

Actual Production History (APH) Example:

A loss occurs when the bushels of soybeans produced for the insurance unit (insurable acreage) fall below the production guarantee as a result of damage from a covered cause of loss. Assumptions: "normal" production = 48 bushels / acre; yield coverage level = 75%; established price coverage = 100%; price election = $9.90 / bushel; actual production = 20 bushels per acre.

48 bushels per acre APH yield
x .75 coverage level
36.0 bushel / acre guarantee

- 20.0 bushels / acre actually produced
16.0 bushels / acre of covered loss x $9.90 per-bushel price election
$158.40 per-acre gross indemnity payment
- $6.00 estimated producer-paid premium per acre (varies)

$152.40 per-acre net indemnity
Revenue Product Example:
36.0 bushels / acre guarantee (see prior example) x $11.00 per-bushel base price (announced in March)
$396.00 per-acre guarantee
20 bushels / acre actually produced
x $10.00 per-bushel harvest price (announced in November)
$200.00 per-acre revenue
$196.00 per-acre gross indemnity payment ($396.00 - $200.00) - $13.00 estimated producer-paid premium (varies)
$183.00 per-acre net indemnity

Source: U.S. Department of Agriculture, Risk Management Agency, 2009 Commodity Insurance Fact Sheet - Soybeans - Iowa, January 2009, http://www.rma.usda.gov/fields/mn_rso/2009/2009iasoybeans.pdf.

Federal Crop Insurance: Range of Coverage and Policies

I. Catastrophic Coverage (CAT) pays 55% of the established price of the commodity on crop losses in excess of 50%. The premium on CAT coverage is paid by the federal government; however, producers must pay a $300 administrative fee for each crop insured in each county. Limited-resource farmers may have this fee waived. CAT coverage is not available on all types of policies.

II. Buy-up Coverage (any coverage level higher than CAT) Yield-based policies:

Actual Production History (APH) and Yield Protection policies insure producers against yield losses due to natural causes such as drought, excessive moisture, hail, wind, frost, insects, and disease. The farmer selects the amount of average yield he or she wishes to insure, from 50% to 85%. The farmer also selects the percentage of the projected price he or she wants to insure—between 55% and 100% of the crop price (for APH, the price is established annually by RMA; for Yield Protection, the price is based on futures market prices).

If the harvest is less than the yield insured, the farmer is paid an indemnity based on the difference. Indemnities are calculated by multiplying this difference by the insured percentage of the selected price.

Area Yield Protection (formerly Group Risk Plan or GRP) insures against widespread loss of production based on county average yields. When the county yield for the insured crop falls below the trigger level selected by the farmer, an indemnity is paid regardless of the individual farmer's actual yield. Yield levels are available for up to 90% of the expected county yield. This protection involves less paperwork and costs less than the farm-level coverage described above. However, individual crop losses may not be covered if the county yield does not suffer a similar loss. This insurance is suitable for farmers whose crop losses typically follow the county pattern.

Dollar Plan provides protection against declining value due to damage that causes a yield shortfall. (Crop examples include cherries, chili peppers, citrus, and nursery crops.) Amount of insurance is based on the cost of growing a crop in a specific area. A loss occurs when the annual crop value is less than the amount of insurance. The maximum dollar amount of insurance is stated on the actuarial document. The insured may select a percentage of the maximum dollar amount equal to CAT (catastrophic level of coverage), or additional coverage levels.

The *Vegetation Index* and *Rainfall Index* do not measure direct production or loss; rather the farmer is insuring against an index that is expected to estimate production. The Pasture, Rangeland, and Forage (PRF) pilot program and the Apiculture pilot program (for beekeepers) use an index for different parts of the country.

Revenue-based policies:

Revenue Protection (RP) insures producers against yield losses due to natural causes such as drought, excessive moisture, hail, wind, frost, insects, and disease, and revenue losses caused by a change in the harvest price from the projected price. The producer selects the amount of average yield he or she wishes to insure, from 50% to 75% (in some areas to 85%). The projected price and the harvest price are 100% of the price determined by futures contracts. The amount of insurance protection is based on the greater of the projected price or the harvest price. If the harvested plus any appraised production multiplied by the harvest price is less than the amount of insurance protection, the producer is paid an indemnity based on the difference.

Revenue Protection With Harvest Price Exclusion insures producers in the same manner as Revenue Protection, except the amount of insurance protection is based on the projected price only (i.e., the amount of insurance protection is not increased if the harvest price is greater than the projected price).

Actual Revenue History (ARH) insures an average of historical grower revenues instead of insuring historical yields as done under APH. Like other revenue coverage plans, ARH protects growers against losses from low yields, low prices, low quality, or any combination of these events.

Area Revenue Protection (formerly Group Risk Income Protection or GRIP) makes indemnity payments only when the average county revenue for the insured crop falls below the revenue guarantee selected by the farmer; Area Revenue Protection with Harvest Price Exclusion is available if upside harvest price protection is not desired.

Adjusted Gross Revenue (AGR) and *AGR-Lite* insure revenue of the entire farm rather than an individual crop by guaranteeing a portion of average gross farm revenue, including a small amount of livestock revenue. The plan uses a producer's Schedule F tax forms, and current-year expected farm revenue, to calculate the guarantee. Beginning in 2015, the Whole-Farm Revenue Protection policy offers a higher coverage level and other enhancements.

Livestock Policies insure against declining market prices or gross margins for swine, cattle, lambs, and milk.

Source: USDA's Risk Management Agency, http://www.rma.usda.gov/policies/.

Revenue-Based Insurance

Revenue insurance accounts for more than half of all crop insurance policies (**Figure 3**). It began in 1997 as a buy-up option on a pilot basis for major crops. By 2003, acreage under revenue-based insurance exceeded acreage covered by yield-based policies.[19]

A "Revenue Protection" policy combines the production guarantee component of crop insurance with a price guarantee to create a target revenue guarantee. Under revenue insurance programs, participating producers are assigned a target level of revenue based on expected market prices for the upcoming season and the producer's yield history. A farmer who opts for revenue insurance can receive an indemnity payment when his actual farm revenue (crop-specific or entire farm, depending on the policy) falls below a certain percentage of the target level of revenue, regardless of whether the shortfall is caused by low prices or low production levels. The price portion of the guarantee rises if the market strengthens between planting and harvest, unless the producer purchases "Revenue Protection With Harvest Price Exclusion." Insurable crops are barley, canola/rapeseed, corn, cotton, grain sorghum, rice, soybeans, sunflowers, and wheat.

For selected other crops such as tart cherries and strawberries, Actual Revenue History (ARH) insures historical revenues and protects growers against losses from low yields, low prices, low quality, or any combination of these events.

Whole Farm Insurance

Adjusted Gross Revenue (AGR) and AGR-Lite policies insure revenue of the entire farm rather than an individual crop. AGR first appeared in 1999 to protect against production or market losses. Compared with AGR, AGR-Lite has higher coverage levels available for producers who have multiple commodities. Both use a producer's five-year historical farm average revenue as reported on the Internal Revenue Service (IRS) tax return form (Schedule F or equivalent forms). Also required is an annual farm report as a base to provide a level of guaranteed revenue for the insurance period (a one-year period corresponding with the producer's IRS tax period). Coverage levels range from 65% to 80% of historical revenue.[20]

In general, the AGR products are designed to protect specialty crops and/or commodities which might not be covered by individual policies. Historically, though, whole-farm insurance has seen limited participation. With individual crop insurance policies already providing significant protection for many producers, combined sales of AGR and AGR-Lite are usually less than 1,000 policies, a small fraction of the more than 1 million crop insurance policies sold. Also, observers say the AGR products are complicated in terms of compiling the information needed to consider purchasing the insurance and completing the application. Others also have noted that for such a policy to be widely adopted, coverage levels need to be substantially higher than individual crop insurance policies (i.e., higher than the current 80% level) in order to provide an amount of risk protection equivalent to that afforded by individual crop policies. A delay in indemnity payment also has been cited by producers as a drawback to those policies.

In response to these concerns, the 2014 farm bill authorized coverage up to 85% and made other enhancements to whole farm insurance. On May 21, 2014, USDA announced that the Whole-Farm Revenue Protection policy would be offered beginning in 2015. The new policy combines Adjusted Gross

Revenue (AGR) and AGR-Lite along with several improvements to target diversified farms and farms selling two to five commodities, including specialty crops to wholesale markets.[21]

Crop Insurance Premium Subsidies

The producer's premium for a policy increases as coverage levels rise, and the premium on buy-up coverage is subsidized by the government at amounts from 38% to 100%, depending on the coverage level (*Table 1*). The subsidy rate declines as the coverage level rises (i.e., deductible declines), but the total subsidy in dollars increases because policies are more expensive.

Table 1. Crop Insurance Premium Subsidies (government-paid portion of premium as a percent of total premium)

Coverage Level (%)	CAT	50	55	60	65	70	75	80	85
Premium subsidy (%) for most polices (including those using basic and optional units)	100	67	64	64	59	59	55	48	38
Premium subsidy (%) for enterprise units	n/a	80	80	80	80	80	77	68	53
Premium subsidy (%) for area plans (yield)	n/a	n/a	n/a	n/a	n/a	59	59	55	55
Premium subsidy (%) for area plans (revenue)	n/a	n/a	n/a	n/a	n/a	59	55	55	49
Premium subsidy (%) for whole farm units	n/a	n/a	n/a	n/a	80	80	80	71	56

Source: 7 U.S.C. §1508(e).

Notes: n/a = not applicable. A basic unit covers land in one county with the same tenant/landlord. An optional unit is a basic unit divided into smaller units by township section. An enterprise unit covers all land of a single crop in a county for a producer, regardless of tenant/landlord structure. A whole farm unit covers more than one crop. For CAT, a loss beyond 50% is indemnified at 55% of the expected price. For coverage level of 50%, a loss beyond that percentage is indemnified at a higher percentage of price (selected by the purchaser) within a minimum and maximum range set by RMA.

Subsidy rates range from 38% to 67% for policies using either "basic" or "optional" units. Basic units cover all plantings in a single county of a crop with the same tenant/landlord. Optional units are basic units divided into smaller units by township section. As authorized under the 2008 farm bill, a higher subsidy rate (up to 80%) is provided for policies using enterprise units (all land for a single crop in a county, regardless of the tenant/landlord structure). Because the premium for policies using enterprise units is lower (a discount is given because the combined unit has greater geographic diversity and hence is less risky), a higher subsidy rate for enterprise units provides for an equal dollar amount of premium subsidy regardless of the type of unit used. Overall, the average subsidy rate was 58% in 2008, 61% in 2009, 62% for 2010 and 2011, 63% in 2012, and 62% in 2013. The rising trend results in part from a shift to policies using enterprise units.

Geographic Distribution of Program Participation and Indemnities

With widespread use of crop insurance products for major crops (corn, cotton, soybeans, and wheat), the geographic distribution of acreage enrolled in crop insurance mirrors that of major producing areas (*Figure 4*). Crop insurance indemnities follow the same pattern, but with an emphasis on producing areas with less rainfall and more variable crop-weather conditions. For example, in 2011, relatively high indemnities were paid in the Great Plains, where drought reduced crop yields in the south and central areas while excessive moisture affected plantings and production in the north.[22] In 2012, a major drought affected a large portion of the United States, and crop insurance indemnities totaled $17.4 billion in 2012, compared with $10.9 billion in 2011 and $4.3 billion in 2010. In 2013, total indemnities declined to $12.0 billion. Losses were significantly lower than the previous year in the Midwest but were extensive across the Plains due to continued drought conditions (*Figure 5*).

Distribution of Producer Subsidies

Producer subsidies for crop insurance are proportional to the value of the premiums and underlying liability of the policies.

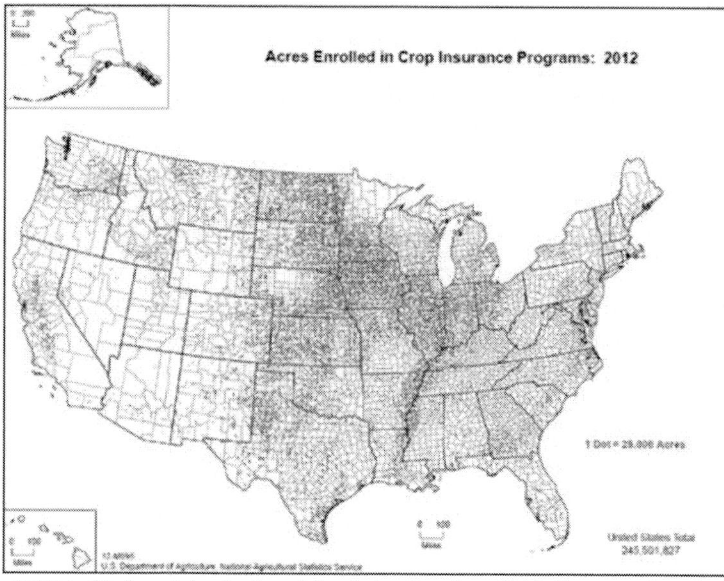

Source: USDA, National Agricultural Statistics Service, 2012 Census of Agriculture.

Figure 4. Acres Enrolled in Crop Insurance, 2012.

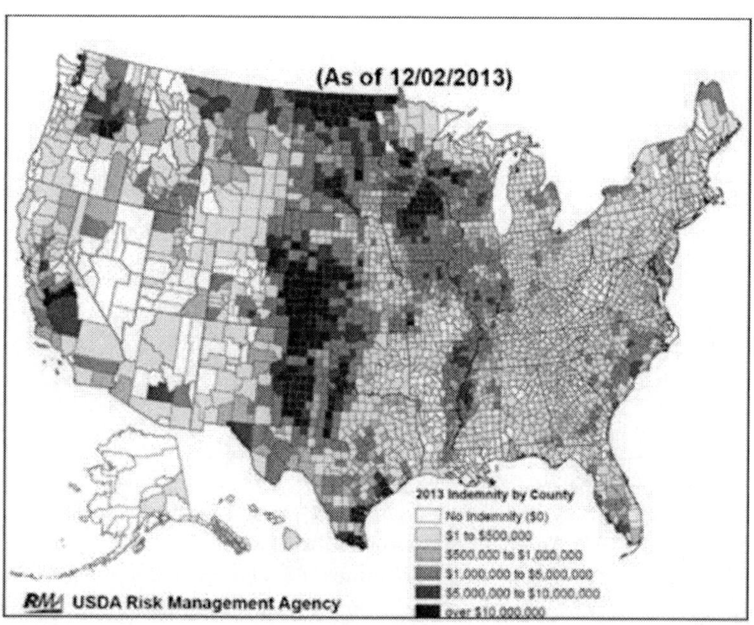

Source: USDA, Risk Management Agency, http://www.rma.usda.gov/data/indemnity/.

Figure 5. Crop Insurance Indemnities in 2013.

Compared with small farms, larger operations have greater crop liability, which increases the total costs of insurance and value of the government-paid portion of the total premium. Based on the distribution of insurance costs from USDA's Agricultural Resource Management Survey (ARMS) and actual premium subsidies from RMA ($5.4 billion in 2009), CRS estimates that the producer subsidy in 2009 averaged nearly $6,000 per farm for farms purchasing crop insurance.[23] By farm size, the calculated average ranged from $1,300 per farm for operations with less than $100,000 in sales to $37,000 for farms with more than $1 million in sales (see *Figure 6*). Unlike farm commodity programs, subsidies received under the crop insurance program are not subject to payment limits.

By crop, the bulk of producer subsidies are for corn, wheat, soybeans, and cotton, which together account for more than 80% of the subsidies and about three-quarters of total acres enrolled in the program (*Figure 7*). By state, premium subsidies are greatest in states where these crops are grown, primarily across the Great Plains, Corn Belt, and parts of the South (*Figure 8*). An analysis by the Government Accountability Office shows a similar geographic distribution for farmers receiving at least $40,000 in producer premium subsidies (*Figure 9*).

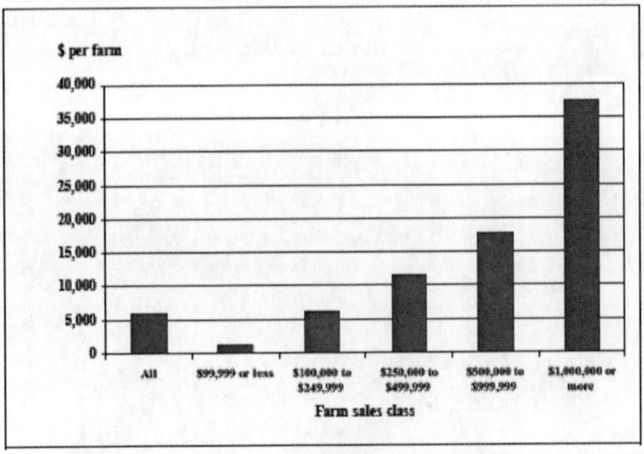

Source: CRS calculation using total premium subsidies from USDA's Risk Management Agency and distribution of crop insurance expenses by farm sales class from USDA's Agricultural Resource Management Survey.

Notes: Total producer subsidy was $5.4 billion for crop year 2009. The calculated average was $5,958 per farm (calculation includes only farms purchasing crop insurance).

Figure 6. Estimated Average Crop Insurance Premium Subsidy Per Farm in 2009.

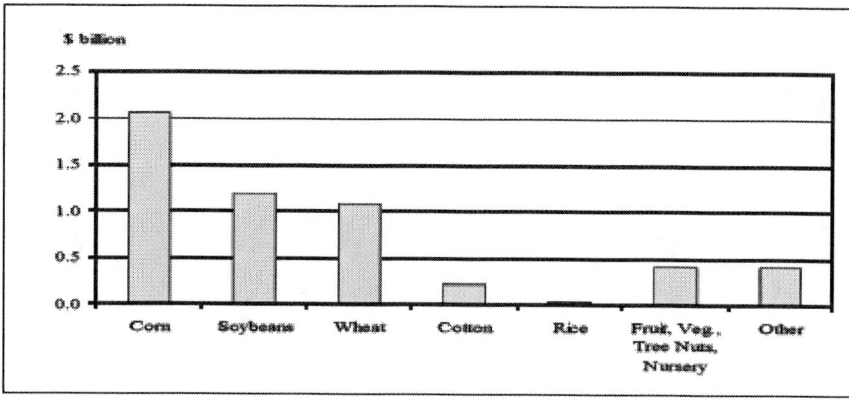

Source: USDA's Risk Management Agency, Summary of Business.

Notes: Total is $5.4 billion in crop year 2009. Corn, soybeans, wheat, and cotton account for 84% of the total.

Other includes minor oilseeds, other feed grains, tobacco, peanuts, sugar beets and sugar cane, pasture, and other crops.

Figure 7. Crop Insurance Premium Subsidies by Crop in 2009.

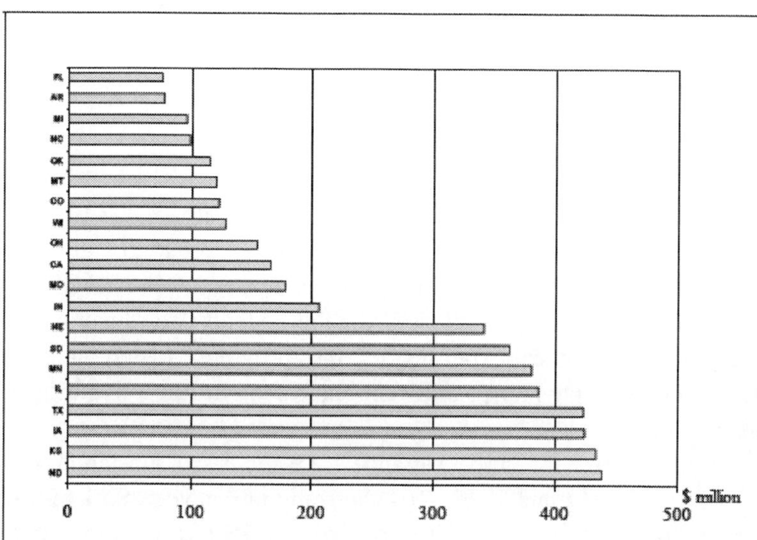

Source: USDA's Risk Management Agency, Summary of Business.

Notes: Total producer subsidy was $5.4 billion in crop year 2009. States in chart accounted for 87% of the total.

Figure 8. Crop Insurance Premium Subsidies for Top 20 States in 2009.

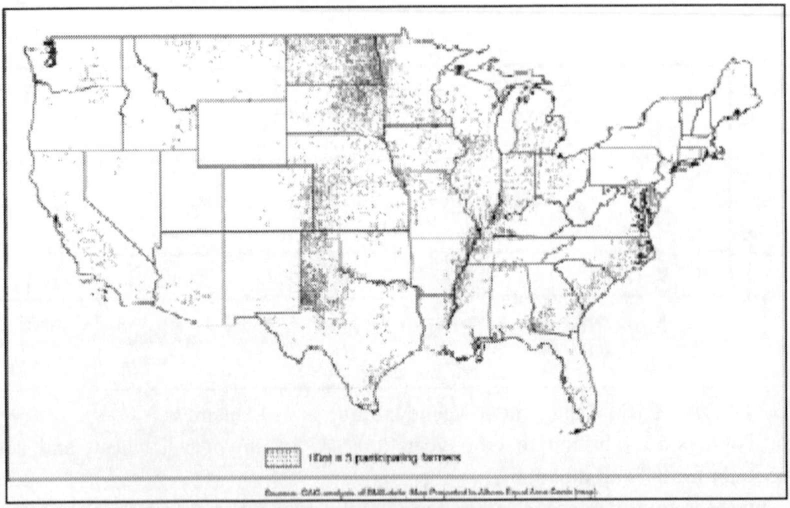

Source: U.S. Government Accountability Office, Crop Insurance: Savings Would Result from Program Changes and Greater Use of Data Mining, GAO-12-256, March 2012, p. 45, http://www.gao.gov/ assets/590/589305.pdf.

Figure 9. Locations of Participating Farmers Receiving Premium Subsidies of More Than $40,000 in 2011.

FEDERAL PROGRAM COSTS

The annual agriculture appropriations bill traditionally makes two separate appropriations for the federal crop insurance program. It provides discretionary funding for the salaries and expenses of the RMA. It also provides "such sums as are necessary" for the Federal Crop Insurance Fund, which finances all other expenses of the program, including premium subsidies, indemnity payments, and reimbursements to the private insurance companies.

Government costs for crop insurance have increased substantially in the last decade (*Figure 10* and *Table 2*). After ranging between $2.1 billion and $3.9 billion during FY2000-FY2007, costs rose to $5.7 billion in FY2008 and $7.0 billion in FY2009 as higher policy premiums from rising crop prices drove up premium subsidies and expense reimbursements to private insurance companies. After a decline in FY2010 following a drop in crop prices and good weather, program costs rose sharply to $11.3 billion in FY2011 and $14.1 billion in FY2012, when crop prices surged again and poor weather resulted in program losses. In FY2013, total program costs declined to $6.0 billion with a return to more favorable weather and smaller crop losses.

The largest cost component is the subsidy on policy premiums for producers, which totaled $7.1 billion in FY2012. Historically, the next largest item is reimbursement of administrative and operating (A&O) expenses to private insurance companies ($1.4 billion in FY2012). With premiums reflecting only costs associated with policy risk, the A&O reimbursement is meant to pay delivery costs. In 4 of the last 10 years, the federal government also has realized underwriting losses (indemnities in excess of premiums received). In the other six years, the government has realized gains, which has partially reduced total costs. The underwriting gains (or losses) are derived in part from the federal government's role in providing the first level of reinsurance—that is, insurance for insurance companies.

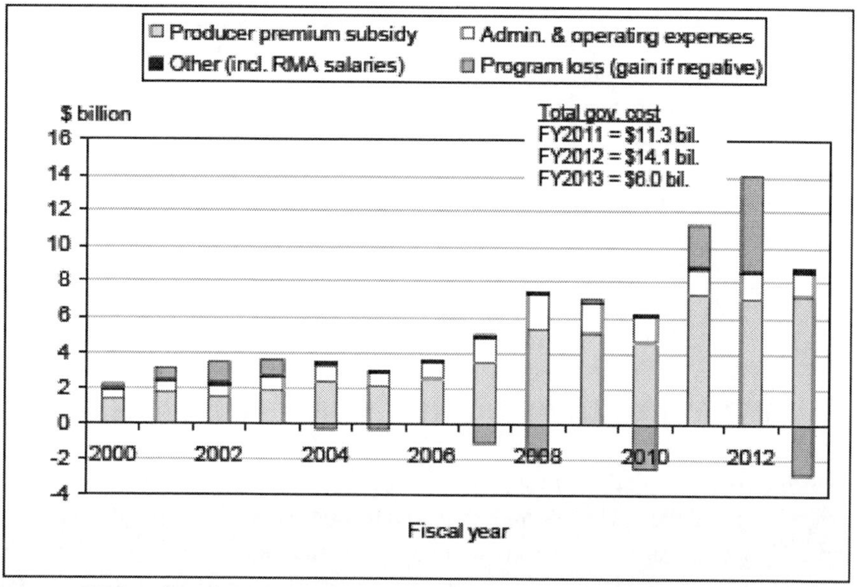

Source: CRS using data from U.S. Department of Agriculture, Risk Management Agency, http://www.rma.usda.gov/aboutrma/budget/costsoutlays.html.

Figure 10. Government Cost of Federal Crop Insurance.

Table 2. Government Cost of Federal Crop Insurance (millions of dollars)

Fiscal Year	Program Losses or (Gains)[a]	Federal Premium Subsidy	Private Company A&O Expense Reimbursements[b]	Other Costsc	Total Government Cost
2004	(305)	2,387	900	143	3,125
2005	(293)	2,070	783	139	2,699
2006	(32)	2,517	960	125	3,570
2007	(1,068)	3,544	1,341	123	3,940
2008	(1,717)	5,301	2,016	137	5,737
2009	108	5,198	1,602	131	7,039
2010	(2,523)	4,680	1,371	143	3,671
2011	2,392	7,376	1,383	144	11,295
2012	5,370	7,149	1,411	141	14,071
2013	(2,827)	7,279	1,350	149	5,951

Source: U.S. Department of Agriculture, Risk Management Agency, http://www.rma.usda.gov/aboutrma/budget/ 13costtable1.pdf.

[A] Government's underwriting loss (gain if negative) = the difference between total indemnity payments for crop losses and total premiums (farmer and government paid), plus or minus any private company underwriting gains or losses.

[B] A&O = administrative and operating.

[C] Other costs include federal salaries of USDA's RMA and, beginning in 2002, various research and development initiatives mandated by the Agriculture Risk Protection Act of 2000 (P.L. 106-224).

Standard Reinsurance Agreement (SRA)

Administrative and operating (A&O) reimbursement to the companies and risk sharing between USDA and the private companies are spelled out in a Standard Reinsurance Agreement (SRA), which plays a large role in determining program costs. The current SRA was completed in summer 2010.[24]

Administrative and Operating (A&O) Reimbursement

Under the current SRA, the calculated reimbursement rate for A&O has been approximately 11% of total premiums since 2011, compared with an average of 19% in 2006-2009.[25] This means that for every $100 in premiums collected, the companies receive a reimbursement of $11 from the federal government. The reimbursement rate varies by insurance product, depending on whether it is for a yield-based or a revenue insurance product.

The SRA places a maximum for A&O reimbursements at $1.3 billion per year (adjusted annually for inflation) and a minimum at $1.1 billion. The cap controls government costs when crop prices rise (price levels directly affect policy premiums), while the minimum is intended to protect companies against low market prices that could reduce reimbursement amounts.

Method for Calculating A&O Reimbursements

Prior to the 2010 renegotiation of the SRA, some observers argued that the reimbursement rate should be pegged to something other than premium value, such as the number of policies sold, to better reflect actual costs and to help reduce federal expenditures. If premiums are actuarially sound, the administrative costs of writing a policy are likely not proportional to the value of the policy (e.g., whether 10 acres or 1,000 acres, or $3 per bushel or $9 per bushel). In order to control costs, A&O reimbursement under the current SRA is still based on premiums (which are directly affected by crop prices), but it is limited to approximately $1.3 billion in 2011 and adjusted upward in subsequent years with an inflation factor. The private crop insurance companies remain concerned that limits on the A&O negatively affects the crop insurance industry and possibly jeopardizes the delivery of crop insurance, particularly in high-risk areas. Part of the criticism of the A&O stemmed from a study by the Government Accountability Office (GAO) on costs associated with administering the crop insurance program.[26] In 2009, GAO concluded that the structure of A&O reimbursements "present[s] an opportunity to reduce government spending without compromising the crop insurance program's safety net for farmers." According to GAO, the method for calculating the A&O reimbursement should be redesigned to better reflect reasonable business expenses, in terms of dollars per policy, rather than crop prices. Using crop prices, GAO said, generated a "kind of windfall" for many insurance agencies/agents as insurance companies, using funds from increased levels of A&O reimbursements, pay higher commissions to compete for each other's "book of business" and associated underwriting gains. In response, the crop insurance industry contended that overall agent compensation was consistent with compensation paid in related insurance industries.

Private Company Risk Sharing

The SRA also defines risk-sharing between the government and private insurance companies. Under the SRA, insurance companies may transfer some liability associated with riskier policies to the government and retain profits/losses from less risky policies.[27] This transfer of risk is accomplished through a set of reinsurance funds maintained by FCIC. Within 30 days of the sales closing dates for each crop, companies allocate each policy they sell to one of two funds that are maintained for each company by state: Assigned Risk or Commercial. Each company then decides what proportion of premiums (and potential for losses/gains) to retain within each reinsurance fund, subject to required retention limits of individual funds. The by-state retention requirements are 20% for the Assigned Risk Fund and at least 35% for the Commercial Fund. The ceded (i.e., not retained) portion of premiums goes to the government.

The assigned risk fund is used for policies believed to be high-risk because it provides the most loss protection to insurance companies through "stop-loss" coverage that reinsures against state-level disasters. For producers, it helps ensure that benefits of the federal crop insurance program are extended to all eligible farmers, regardless of risk. Because companies retain only 20% of their business as specified in the SRA, the federal government assumes a large portion of liability associated with high-risk policies. The SRA also specifies a 75% limit (by state) on the proportion of a company's business that may be placed in the Assigned Risk Fund.

The Commercial Fund is for policies that the companies expect to have the greatest opportunity for profit and only a small amount of losses. While the profit potential is greater compared with the Assigned Risk Fund, so is the loss potential.

Once the policies are allocated to one of the two funds, the gain/loss sharing for a company's retained business is based on loss ratios (indemnities paid divided by premiums collected) as established in the SRA. As a general rule, the higher the loss ratio, the lower the company share of gains or losses (and vice versa, except at very low loss ratios when the company share of gains declines). See *Table 3* for the schedule contained in the current SRA. *Figure 11* illustrates risk sharing for the Commercial Fund.

For the Commercial Fund, policies sold in states with historically lower underwriting gains have a more favorable gain/loss sharing structure for insurance companies than policies sold in five states with better underwriting performance (Illinois, Indiana, Iowa, Minnesota, and Nebraska). The provision is designed to provide insurance companies with more financial incentives than in the past to sell and service policies in the areas of the country that have historically attracted less interest because companies had expected fewer underwriting gains in those areas.

The final risk-sharing component of the SRA is the "net book quota share," defined as the proportion of a company's overall gain or loss over its entire "book of business" that is ceded to the government after all other reinsurance provisions in the SRA have been applied. Under the SRA, companies must cede a 6.5% share of their cumulative underwriting gains/losses to the government. During years in which there are underwriting gains, 1.5% of this share is distributed back to companies that sell and service policyholders in 17 underserved states. Through the net book quota share, the government receives a portion of underwriting gains from a company's retained business (but will also pay a portion of the losses, if realized). Since the company's total book includes a higher proportion of policies with lower risk, this portion is generally a positive value, which offsets part of the government costs of the program.

Table 3. Share of Crop Insurance Company's Gains/Losses by Fund and Loss Ratio (share of gains/losses in percent)

Loss Ratio (%)	Share of Company's Gains/Losses in Assigned Risk Fund (%)	Share of Company's Gains/Losses in Commercial Fund (%)	
		Group1 (IL, IN, IA, MN, NE)	All other states
0 to 50	3	5	5
>50 to 65	13.5	40	40
>65 to 100	22.5	75	97.5
>100 to 160	7.5	65	42.5
>160 to 220	6	45	20
>220 to 500	3	10	5
>500	0	0	0

Source: U.S. Department of Agriculture, Risk Management Agency, Standard Reinsurance Agreement dated June 30, 2010, http://www.rma.usda.gov/news/2010/06/630sra.pdf.

Notes: Loss ratio is indemnities divided by total premiums. See figure on risk sharing for illustration.

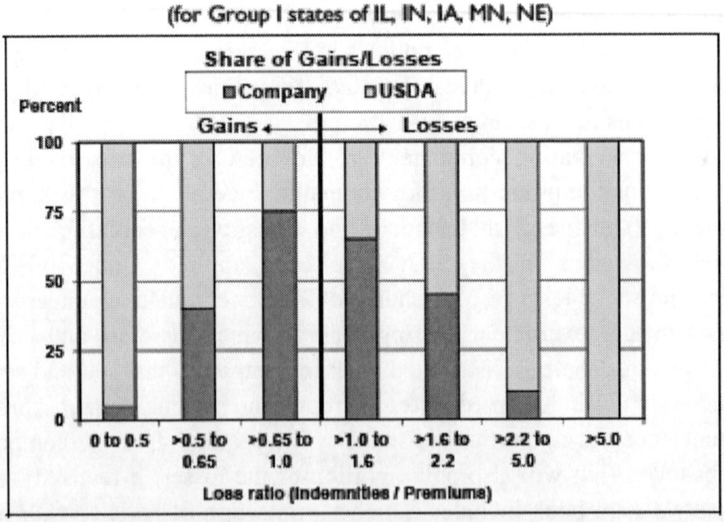

Source: CRS, using data from U.S. Department of Agriculture, Risk Management Agency, Standard Reinsurance Agreement dated June 30, 2010, http://www.rma.usda.gov/news/2010/06/630sra.pdf.

Notes: The USDA share of gains and losses is lowest when the loss ratio (indemnities divided by premiums) is near 1.0. Insurance companies place "less risky" policies in the Commercial Fund. Separate schedules apply to the Commercial Fund in all other states and for the Assigned Risk Fund (higher risk policies).

Figure 11. Risk Sharing for the Commercial Fund.

Trends in A&O Reimbursement and Underwriting Gains

Since A&O reimbursements are based on a percentage of premiums, the dollar amount of A&O reimbursement increased sharply during the late 2000s as premiums rose, reflecting higher crop prices. The A&O reimbursement increased from an average of $881 million during 2004-2006 to $2.0 billion in 2008 (*Table 2*). A&O reimbursements declined to $1.6 billion in FY2009 following a decline in crop prices. Under changes in the 2010 SRA, an inflation-adjusted cap has limited annual A&O expenditures to about $1.4 billion. Company underwriting gains (the amount by which a company's share of retained premiums exceeds its indemnities) increased substantially during the 2000s as weather was generally favorable for crops (*Table 4*). In 2012, though, a major drought across major producing regions led to sharply higher indemnities, which resulted in large losses for the 2012 crop year. More favorable weather returned in 2013, which reduced indemnities and generated an underwriting gain for the insurance companies.

During the last decade, increases in insured acreage and higher crop prices have also increased gross liability. Liability represents total exposure of the program, meaning that if all participating farmers suffer losses to the full extent of coverage, indemnities would be the total liability.

Table 4. Federal Crop Insurance Program and Company Data

Crop Year	Net Acres Insured (mil. acres)	Gross Premium[a] ($ million)	Gross Liability[b] ($ million)	Gross Loss Ratio[c]	Private Co. Underwriting Gain (Loss)[d] ($ million)
2004	221	4,186	46,602	0.79	696
2005	246	3,949	44,259	0.60	915
2006	242	4,580	49,919	0.77	825
2007	272	6,562	67,340	0.54	1,574
2008	273	9,851	89,893	0.88	1,098
2009	265	8,951	79,572	0.58	2,277
2010	256	7,594	78,102	0.56	1,929
2011	266	11,970	114,201	0.91	1,666
2012	283	11,113	117,153	1.57	(1,317)
2013 (est.)	296	11,783	123,411	1.01	661

Source: For premium, liability, and loss ratio, Summary of Business Report, FCIC, http://www.rma.usda.gov/data/ sob.html. For underwriting gain/loss, Crop Year Premium and Other Income, FCIC, http://www.rma.usda.gov/ aboutrma/budget/ 2013cyprem.pdf. Estimate for 2013 current as of May 2014.

[a] Farmer-paid premium plus government-paid premium subsidy.

[b] Liability represents total exposure of the program, meaning that if all participating farmers suffered losses to the full extent of coverage, program indemnities would be the total liability.

[c] Indemnities divided by premiums. Gross loss ratio is for the program in total (government plus private companies).

[d] The underwriting gains represent the amount by which the company's share of retained premiums exceeds its indemnities (vice versa for underwriting losses).

CROP INSURANCE IN THE 2014 FARM BILL

The federal crop insurance program is permanently authorized. Hence, periodic reauthorization of the program, including premium subsidies, is not needed, unlike farm commodity programs that are enacted under traditional "farm bills." The 2014 farm bill (P.L. 113-79) authorized farm programs for the years 2014-2018 and made a number of permanent changes to the federal crop insurance program.[28]

A prominent crop insurance feature of the 2014 farm bill is the authorization of policies designed to reimburse "shallow losses"—an insured producer's out-of-pocket loss associated with the policy deductible. A new crop insurance policy called Stacked Income Protection Plan (STAX) is made available for upland cotton producers, while the Supplemental Coverage Option (SCO) is made available for other crops. The STAX policy indemnifies losses in county revenue of greater than 10% of expected revenue but not more than the deductible level (e.g., 25%) selected by the producer for the underlying individual policy. (It can also be purchased as a stand-alone policy.) Similarly, SCO is based on expected county revenue (or yields) and covers part of the deductible under the producer's underlying policy. The government subsidy as a share of the policy premium is set at 80% for STAX and 65% for SCO.

A variety of additional farm bill provisions expand existing crop insurance products or require examination of the potential for new products, including those that would benefit specialty crops and animal agriculture. Provisions revise the value of crop insurance for organic crops to reflect generally higher prices of organic (not conventional) crops. USDA is also required to conduct more research on whole farm revenue insurance with higher coverage levels than currently available. Studies or policies are also required for insuring (1) producers of specialty crops (e.g., fruits, vegetables) for food safety and contamination-related losses, (2) swine producers for a catastrophic disease event, (3) producers of catfish against reduction in the margin between market prices and production costs, (4) commercial poultry production against business disruptions caused by integrator bankruptcy, (5) poultry producers for a catastrophic event, (6) producers of biomass sorghum or sweet sorghum grown as feedstock for renewable energy, and (7) alfalfa producers. A peanut revenue insurance product and rice margin insurance also are mandated. Another provision provides funding for index weather insurance for protecting against weather conditions that deviate from average levels.

To address conservation concerns, the 2014 farm bill links eligibility for crop insurance premium subsidies to compliance with wetland and conservation requirements for highly erodible land. Also, crop insurance subsidies are reduced for plantings on native sod acreage in certain states.

Despite calls by critics of the program to reduce federal funding, the crop insurance title of the farm bill increased total funding for the program by an additional $5.7 billion over 10 years relative to projected levels that assumed no change in policy. The largest cost items were STAX ($3.3 billion) and SCO ($1.7 billion), according to the Congressional Budget Office. The cost of expanding the crop insurance program was offset by the elimination of fixed "direct" payments, denoting a policy shift from farm payments made regardless of market conditions to enhanced risk management programs. A controversial item not included in P.L. 113-79 was the reduction of premium subsidies for high-income farmers, which had been included in the Senate farm bill but not the House bill.

CONCLUDING COMMENTS

For many farmers, crop insurance is the most important component of the farm safety net, given the loss protection it affords and the large number of crops that are covered. The program generally has widespread support among farm-state legislators and Members of the agriculture committees where farm policy is developed. During the debate that shaped the 2014 farm bill, critics of crop insurance vigorously attempted but were not successful in reducing the scope and benefits of the federal crop insurance program, including premium subsidy levels and reimbursements to private insurance companies.

Federal outlays for crop insurance exceed those for commodity programs, making crop insurance the most costly component of the farm safety net and a potential target for legislators looking for cost offsets to pay for other legislation or for deficit reduction. For policy makers, a main goal when contemplating future modifications to the crop insurance program would likely be saving federal dollars without adversely affecting farmer participation or policy coverage that might result in calls for ad hoc disaster assistance. A concern from the industry is that any cuts could adversely affect company interest in selling and servicing crop insurance to farmers, although some say that compensation is more than adequate. Separately, environmental groups are concerned that premium subsidies might encourage production on environmentally fragile land.

End Notes

[1] For more on the history of federal crop insurance, see http://www.rma.usda.gov/aboutrma/what/history.html. Law citations are the Federal Crop Insurance Act of 1980 (P.L. 96-365), the Federal Crop Insurance Reform Act of 1994 (P.L. 103-354), and the Agriculture Risk Protection Act (ARPA) of 2000 (P.L. 106-224). Additional background on the program's rationale is available the following three articles: (1) Joseph W. Glauber, "The Growth of the Federal Crop Insurance Program, 1990-2011," Amer. J. Agr. Econ., vol. 95, no. 2 (January 2013), pp. 482-488; (2) Keith H. Coble and Barry J. Barnett, "Why Do We Subsidize Crop Insurance?," Amer. J. Agr. Econ., vol. 95, no. 2 (January 2013), pp. 498-504; and (3) Barry K. Goodwin and Vincent H, Smith, "What Harm Is Done by Subsidizing Crop Insurance?," Amer. J. Agr. Econ., vol. 95, no. 2 (January 2013), pp. 489-497.

[2] CRS Report R43494, Crop Insurance Provisions in the 2014 Farm Bill (P.L. 113-79).

[3] In practice, the crop insurance company bills the farmer for the producer's portion of the premium (i.e., excluding the government portion). The company then sends the entire producer-paid premium to RMA. When a producer files a claim and the company pays an indemnity, RMA reimburses the company in full for the loss. At the end of the reinsurance year, there is an annual settlement whereby the company's proportion of any underwriting gain or loss is determined and paid.

[4] Insured percentage is for 2011. For a detailed analysis by crop, see USDA Risk Management Agency, The Risk Management Safety Net: Portfolio Analysis-Market Penetration and Potential, Washington, DC, August 2013, http://www.rma.usda.gov/pubs/2013/portfolio/portfolio.pdf.

[5] A complete list of 2014 crops is available at http://www.rma.usda.gov/policies/ 2014 policy.html.

[6] Carey Frick, "Frick: Not So Peachy," The State, May 26, 2010.

[7] USDA Risk Management Agency, The Risk Management Safety Net: Portfolio Analysis-Market Penetration and Potential, Washington, DC, August 2013, http://www.rma.usda.gov/pubs/2013/portfolio/portfolio.pdf. For additional information, see Federal Crop Insurance Corporation, Report to Congress: Specialty Crop Report, Washington, DC, November 2010, http://www.rma.usda.gov/pubs/2010/specialtycrop.pdf.

[8] For descriptions of Livestock Gross Margin (margin protection) and Livestock Risk Protection (price protection), see http://www.rma.usda.gov/livestock/.

[9] For more information, see http://www.rma.usda.gov/policies/pasturerangeforage/. Also see Monte Vandeveer, Pasture, Rangeland, and Forage Insurance: A Risk Management Tool for Hay and Livestock Producers, University of Nebraska-Lincoln, October 2012, http://cropwatch. unl.edu/c/document_library/get_file?uuid=3f25e3ef-68d1-4489- a7dd-7daba3c2d385&groupId=1841&.pdf.

[10] For a description of the program, see http://www.rma.usda.gov/policies/ri-vi/annualforage.html.

[11] A list of RMA regional offices is available at http://www.rma.usda.gov/aboutrma/ fields/rsos.html.

[12] For more information, see USDA, Risk Management Agency, Requesting Insurance Not Available in Your County, Program Aid 1929, September 2013, http://www.rma.usda.gov/pubs/rme/requestinginsurance.pdf. See also the FCIC "Written Agreement Handbook," http://www.rma.usda.gov/handbooks/24000/2013/24020.pdf.

[13] For more information on NAP, see the USDA fact sheet at http://fsa.usda.gov/Internet/FSA_File/nap09.pdf.

[14] Growers have expressed a preference for no development of insurance products for a number of crops; see Attachment 2 in USDA Risk Management Agency, The Risk Management Safety Net: Portfolio Analysis-Market Penetration and Potential, Washington, DC, August 2013, http://www.rma.usda.gov/pubs/2013/portfolio/portfolio.pdf.

[15] U.S. Department of Agriculture, Risk Management Agency, http://www.rma.usda.gov/help/faq/basics.html.

[16] For a detailed discussion, see U.S. Department of Agriculture, Risk Management Agency, Premium Rate Adjustment, November 2012, http://www.rma.usda.gov/news/2012/11/2013premiumrateadjustment.pdf.

[17] A number of university and Extension Service offices provide information to farmers when making crop insurance decisions. Some examples include http://www.agmanager.info/crops/insurance/risk_mgt/default.asp, http://www. ag.ndsu.nodak.edu/aginfo/cropmkt/cic.htm, and http://www.farmdoc.uiuc.edu/cropins/index.asp.

[18] Participation at the CAT level has steadily decreased, particularly since subsidies on buy-up levels were increased in the Agriculture Risk Protection Act (ARPA) of 2000. In 2011, only about 11% of insured acres were insured at the CAT level.

[19] After years of development, USDA's Risk Management Agency issued the "COMBO" rule in late March 2010 to consolidate several crop insurance plans into a single "Common Crop Insurance Policy" beginning with the 2011 crop year. The biggest change was the consolidation of several previous revenue products (Crop Revenue Coverage, Income Protection, Indexed Income Protection, and Revenue Assurance) into a single revenue product called Revenue Protection. See USDA, Risk Management Agency, "RMA Releases New Common Crop Insurance Policy Basic Provisions," press release, March 31, 2010, http://www.rma.usda.gov/news/2010/03/combo.html.

[20] For more information, see USDA fact sheet at http://www.rma.usda.gov/pubs/rme/agr-lite.pdf.

[21] U.S. Department of Agriculture, "New Pilot Program Offers Coverage for Fruits and Vegetables, Organic and Diversified Farms," press release, May 21, 2014, http://www.usda.gov/wps/portal/usda/usdamediafb?contentid=2014/05/0100.xml&printable=true&contentidonly=true.

[22] Adverse weather can affect crops in various ways. For example, in some North Dakota counties in 2009, the cause of loss was drought for some wheat policies, while it was excess moisture for other wheat policies in the same county.

[23] The producer subsidy in 2009 averaged $2,500 per farm when the calculation includes all U.S. farms, not just those purchasing crop insurance. By farm size, the calculated average ranged from $400 per farm for operations with less than $100,000 in sales to $32,000 for farms with more than $1 million in sales.

[24] As authorized by the 2008 farm bill, USDA may renegotiate the SRA once every five years starting with the 2011 reinsurance year (the 12-month period beginning July 1, 2010). For more information on the SRA and related issues, see CRS Report R40966, Renegotiation of the Standard Reinsurance Agreement (SRA) for Federal Crop Insurance.

[25] The 2008 farm bill (§12016(E)) reduced the A&O reimbursement by 2.3 percentage points beginning with the 2009 reinsurance year (July 1, 2008). Also, the farm bill reduced the A&O reimbursement rate to 12% for any plan of insurance that is based on area-wide losses. The farm bill also reduced the target loss ratio (indemnities paid divided by premiums collected of the entire program) from 1.075 to 1.00.

26 U.S. Government Accountability Office, Crop Insurance—Opportunities Exist to Reduce the Costs of Administering the Program, Washington, DC, April 2009, http://www.gao.gov/new.items/d09445.pdf.

[27] Dmitry V. Vedenov et al., "Portfolio Allocation and Alternative Structures of the Standard Reinsurance Agreement," vol. 31, no. 1 (April 2006), pp. 57-73, http://ageconsearch.umn.edu/bitstream/10145/1/31010057.pdf. See also Joseph W. Glauber, "Crop Insurance Reconsidered," American Journal of Agricultural Economics, vol. 86, no. 5 (2004), pp. 1179-1195.

[28] For more information, see CRS Report R43494, Crop Insurance Provisions in the 2014 Farm Bill (P.L. 113-79).

In: Federal Crop Insurance
Editor: Tristan E. Bonner ISBN: 978-1-63463-688-9

Chapter 2

CROP INSURANCE PROVISIONS IN THE 2014 FARM BILL (P.L. 113-79)*

Dennis A. Shields

SUMMARY

The enacted 2014 farm bill (the Agricultural Act of 2014; P.L. 113-79) enhances the federal crop insurance program by expanding its scope, covering a greater share of farm losses, and making other modifications that broaden policy coverage. The changes stem from the desire of many in Congress, particularly members of the agriculture committees, to bolster what they consider to be the most significant aspect of the farm safety net.

Under the federal crop insurance program, which is administered by the U.S. Department of Agriculture's Risk Management Agency (RMA), producers purchase subsidized policies to help manage financial risks associated with crop yield or revenue losses, primarily from natural disasters. In contrast, farm commodity programs apply to a narrower set of "program" crops, require no participation fees, and make payments when prices fall below statutory minimums or when crop revenue is low relative to historical levels.

A prominent crop insurance feature of the 2014 farm bill is the authorization of policies designed to reimburse "shallow losses"—an

---

* This is an edited, reformatted and augmented version of a Congressional Research Service publication R43494, prepared for Members and Committees of Congress dated April 22, 2014.

insured producer's out-of-pocket loss associated with the policy deductible. A new crop insurance policy called Stacked Income Protection Plan (STAX) is made available for upland cotton producers, while the Supplemental Coverage Option (SCO) is made available for other crops. The STAX policy indemnifies losses in county revenue of greater than 10% of expected revenue but not more than the deductible level (e.g., 25%) selected by the producer for the underlying individual policy. (It can also be purchased as a stand-alone policy.) Similarly, SCO is based on expected county revenue (or yields) and covers part of the deductible under the producer's underlying policy. The government subsidy as a share of the policy premium is set at 80% for STAX and 65% for SCO.

A variety of additional provisions are expected to expand existing crop insurance products or require examination of the potential for new products, including those that would benefit specialty crops and animal agriculture. Provisions revise the value of crop insurance for organic crops to reflect generally higher prices of organic (not conventional) crops. USDA is also required to conduct more research on whole farm revenue insurance with higher coverage levels than currently available. Studies or policies are also required for insuring (1) specialty crop producers for food safety and contamination-related losses, (2) swine producers for a catastrophic disease event, (3) producers of catfish against reduction in the margin between the market prices and production costs, (4) commercial poultry production against business disruptions caused by integrator bankruptcy, (5) poultry producers for a catastrophic event, (6) producers of biomass sorghum or sweet sorghum grown as feedstock for renewable energy, and (7) alfalfa producers. A peanut revenue insurance product and rice margin insurance also are mandated. Another provision provides funding for index weather insurance for protecting against weather.

To address conservation concerns, the 2014 farm bill links eligibility for crop insurance premium subsidies to compliance with wetland and conservation requirements for highly erodible land. Also, crop insurance subsidies are reduced for plantings on native sod acreage in certain states.

In total, the crop insurance title increases funding for crop insurance by an additional $5.7 billion over 10 years relative to projected levels that assumed no change in policy. The largest cost items are for STAX ($3.3 billion) and SCO ($1.7 billion), according to the Congressional Budget Office. A controversial item not included in P.L. 113-79 was the reduction of premium subsidies for high-income farmers, which had been included in the Senate farm bill but not the House bill.

INTRODUCTION

The federal crop insurance program is considered by many farmers and policy makers as the centerpiece of the farm safety net. The program makes available subsidized insurance policies for about 130 commodities ranging from apples to wheat. These "multiple peril" policies help producers manage financial risks associated with crop yield or revenue losses. Insurable causes of losses include adverse weather (e.g., drought and flood), insects or disease outbreaks, and failure of irrigation water supply.

The enacted 2014 farm bill (the Agricultural Act of 2014; P.L. 113-79) enhances the federal crop insurance program by expanding its scope, covering a greater share of farm losses, and making a variety of other modifications that broaden policy coverage. This report describes in detail changes made to the program as part of the 2014 farm bill. A table at the end of this report (*Table A-1*) provides a side-by-side comparison of the crop insurance provisions in Title XI of the 2014 farm bill and the permanent authorizing statute for federal crop insurance (Federal Crop Insurance Act, 7 U.S.C. §1501 et seq.), prior to enactment of the 2014 farm bill.

Two other key elements of the farm safety net are (1) the farm commodity programs, which provide price and income support for a much narrower list of "covered and loan commodities" such as corn, soybeans, wheat, rice, and peanuts; and (2) agricultural disaster programs, which primarily assist producers owning livestock or fruit trees.

CROP INSURANCE BACKGROUND[1]

Policy Rationale for Federal Crop Insurance

In 1938, Congress established the federal crop insurance program following several unsuccessful attempts by the private sector to sell multiple-peril policies, beginning in the late 1800s.[2] These ventures lost money and were discontinued because areas they covered were too small to adequately distribute risks when crops failed. Since then, private crop insurance has focused on single peril insurance for causes of loss not correlated across wide areas, such as hail or fire.[3]

Agricultural weather risks typically affect a large area rather than individual farms, resulting in potential losses that historically have been considered too large for private insurers. Others, though, contend that international financial markets have expanded dramatically in recent decades and now have significant capacity to provide coverage of risks that are much greater than those associated with potential crop losses.[4]

Separately, the crop insurance program must address problems associated with moral hazard, such as farmers intentionally under-applying crop inputs to collect indemnities. Another issue is adverse selection, whereby high-risk farmers tend to participate more than low-risk farmers, thus increasing program costs. Some argue that the government is in a better position than the private sector to address these issues and monitor farm behavior and losses given better access to data and linkages with farm program benefits.

From a demand standpoint, federal subsidies for purchasing crop insurance have been increased over the years to improve affordability and boost farmer participation.[5] In general, the premium required to cover the cost of crop insurance is more than producers are willing to pay. As a result, in the absence of federal subsidies, U.S. agricultural acreage covered by crop insurance and coverage levels selected by farmers would likely be lower, potentially increasing the odds of a costly federal bailout in the event of a catastrophic weather event.

Proponents of federal crop insurance argue that the program is essential because it provides specific risk management solutions that benefit farmers, input suppliers, the entire agricultural sector, and ultimately all food consumers. They also say widespread participation reduces the potential for ad-hoc disaster spending, a longstanding policy goal. In contrast, critics argue that the program covers an excessive amount of producer risk, inappropriately subsidizes large farms, wastes taxpayer dollars, and encourages crop production on environmentally fragile lands.

Authorizing Legislation

The federal crop insurance program is permanently authorized by the Federal Crop Insurance Act, as amended (7 U.S.C. §1501 et seq.). The Federal Crop Insurance Corporation (FCIC) was created as a wholly-owned government corporation in 1938 to carry out the program. The program is administered by the U.S. Department of Agriculture's Risk Management Agency (RMA).

Insurable Commodities and Types of Policies

Policies are available for approximately 130 crops and cover more than 250 million acres nationwide. Insurable commodities include major field crops such as wheat, corn, soybeans, cotton, peanuts, and rice, as well as many specialty crops (including fruit, tree nut, vegetable, and nursery crops), pasture, rangeland, and forage crops.[6] For major crops, three-fourths or more of U.S. planted acreage is insured under the federal crop insurance program.

Farmers annually purchase about 1.2 million policies, with many producers purchasing multiple policies depending on farm size and number of crops grown. The policies protect against individual farm losses in yield, crop revenue, or whole farm revenue. Area-wide policies are available for some crops, whereby an indemnity is paid when there is an overall loss over a broad area level. In general, yield-based policies offer a guarantee at the individual farm level or area-wide (e.g., county) level. For revenue policies, the insurance guarantee also incorporates the expected market price prior to planting (i.e., no statutory minimum prices as provided in some farm programs). For some policies, the guarantee can increase if the harvest price is higher than the expected price, thereby increasing the point at which indemnities are triggered.

The producer selects a coverage level and absorbs the initial loss through the deductible. For example, a coverage level of 70% has a 30% deductible (for a total equal to 100% of the expected value prior to planting the crop). The producer pays a portion of the premium which increases as the level of coverage rises. The federal government pays the rest of the premium—62%, on average, in 2013—plus the cost of selling and servicing the policies. This differs from farm commodity programs, which require no participation fees. Also unlike farm commodity programs, crop insurance has no subsidy limits, and participants can be eligible regardless of income levels.

Program Structure and Federal Costs

The federal crop insurance program is a partnership between RMA (through the FCIC) and private industry. RMA approves and supports products, develops and approves the premium rates, administers premium subsidies, reimburses private companies for their administrative and operating costs (i.e., delivery costs for selling and servicing the policies), and reinsures company losses. RMA also sponsors educational and outreach programs and seminars on the general topic of risk management.

Approximately 19 private insurance companies provide the "boots on the ground" for selling and servicing the insurance policies through a network of agents. They also share risk (profit/loss potential) with the government. The Standard Reinsurance Agreement (SRA) defines the risk-sharing arrangement, whereby insurance companies may transfer some liability associated with riskier policies to the federal government and retain profits/losses from less risky policies.[7]

During FY2009-FY2013, federal costs averaged $8.4 billion per year, varying between $3.7 billion in FY2010 and $14.1 billion in FY2012, depending on crop losses and commodity prices, which affect premium subsidy amounts and program liability (e.g., high market price result in high premiums and liability).

CROP INSURANCE PROVISIONS IN THE 2014 FARM BILL

The general enhancement of the federal crop insurance program in the 2014 farm bill stems from the desire of many in Congress, particularly members of the agriculture committees, to bolster what they consider to be the most significant aspect of the farm safety net. Unlike farm commodity programs, federal crop insurance is applicable to a wide variety of crops and requires producers to pay for at least part of the program. Producers are indemnified only after an insurable crop loss. During the farm bill debate, some in Congress voiced concerns that the program is too generous. Congress considered but did not pass premium caps and/or income limits on crop insurance similar to ones governing farm commodity program payments.

For crop insurance in the 2014 farm bill, a prominent feature is the authorization of policies designed to reimburse "shallow losses"—an insured producer's out-of-pocket loss associated with the policy deductible. These include a new crop insurance policy called Stacked Income Protection Plan (STAX) for upland cotton and the Supplemental Coverage Option (SCO) for other crops. A variety of additional provisions are expected to expand existing crop insurance products or require FCIC to examine the potential for new products, including those benefiting specialty crops and animal agriculture.

Stacked Income Protection Plan (STAX) for Upland Cotton

Beginning with the 2014 farm bill, upland cotton is no longer a "covered commodity," making upland cotton producers ineligible for either Price Loss Coverage (PLC) or Agriculture Risk Coverage (ARC) under the farm commodity support programs. Instead, upland cotton is eligible for Stacked Income Protection (STAX), which is a revenue-based, area-wide crop insurance policy that may be purchased as a stand-alone policy for primary coverage or purchased in tandem with an individual farm loss policy or area policy. This major policy revision was sought by U.S. cotton producers in an attempt to resolve a long-running trade dispute with Brazil that requires changing the U.S. cotton support program so it does not distort international markets.[8]

Critical to participation, and as part of the agreement to make upland cotton ineligible for the PLC/ARC programs, is the government's share of the premium cost. The federal subsidy is 80% for STAX and the government pays for delivery costs. Policies are to be offered in all producing counties at the county level, or on the basis of a larger geographic area if necessary. A payment rate multiplier of 120% is available if producers want to increase the amount of protection per acre.

The indemnity from STAX is triggered by a revenue loss at the county level. When purchased as a "stacked" policy, the indemnity is designed to cover part of the deductible of the underlying policy. Specifically, STAX would indemnify losses in county revenue of greater than 10% of expected revenue but not more than 30%.[9] For producers purchasing STAX in conjunction with an individual policy, the maximum coverage under STAX cannot exceed the deductible level selected by the producer in the underlying individual policy. For individual producers, indemnities for STAX and other policies cannot overlap.

A graphical illustration of STAX is shown *Figure 1*. The bar on the left depicts the expected revenue (prior to planting) under a typical cotton crop insurance revenue policy with a 30% deductible (the farmer absorbs the first 30% of the loss). The expected revenue is the 10-year average yield for an individual producer times the expected market price (the average futures market price prior to planting). The insurance guarantee is set at 70% of the expected revenue (100% minus the 30% deductible). Upon harvest, if actual revenue falls short of the guarantee, an initial indemnity is triggered under the farmer's individual crop insurance policy as depicted by the green box in the right-hand column. If a STAX policy is also purchased and there is a loss at the county level, a STAX indemnity would be paid (depicted by the blue box). Overall, the farmer incurs a loss of approximately 10% (white box at top), with the STAX indemnity reducing the amount of "shallow loss" absorbed by the producer.

(STAX for upland cotton covers part of the deductible under the individual policy)

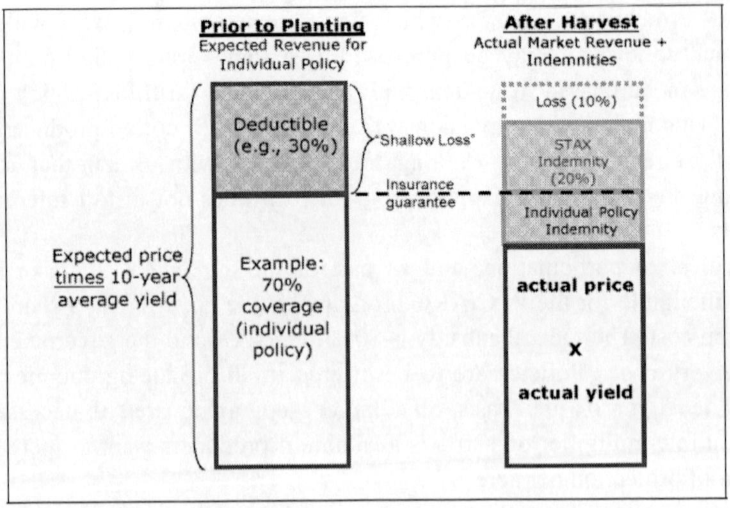

Source: CRS.

Notes: A STAX indemnity (blue box above) is triggered when actual county revenue is less than 90% of expected county revenue. Scenario assumes expected (and actual) revenue is the same at the individual farm and county level (STAX). STAX may be purchased as a stand-alone policy for primary coverage. Upland cotton acres enrolled in STAX are not eligible for SCO.

Figure 1. Stacked Income Protection Plan (STAX) with a Crop Loss.

Supplemental Coverage Option (SCO)

Like STAX but for other crops, the Supplemental Coverage Option (SCO) is authorized by the 2014 farm bill to cover part of the deductible under the producer's underlying policy (the "shallow loss"). SCO is an area-wide (e.g., county) loss policy, whereby an indemnity is paid on area losses not more than the deductible level (e.g., 25%) selected by the producer for the underlying individual policy. However, unlike STAX, the SCO guarantee can be based on either expected county yields or revenue, and it must be purchased in conjunction with a traditional crop insurance policy. Indemnities are triggered by county losses greater than 14%, and policy coverage cannot exceed the difference between 86% and the coverage level selected by the producer for the underlying policy.

A graphical illustration of SCO is shown in *Figure 2.*[10] The bar on the left depicts the expected revenue (prior to planting) under a typical crop insurance revenue policy with a 30% deductible (the farmer absorbs the first 30% of the loss). The expected revenue is the 10-year average yield for a producer times the expected market price (e.g., average futures market price for major crops). The guarantee is set at 70% of the expected revenue (100% minus the 30% deductible). If a loss occurs on the farm, an initial indemnity is triggered under the farmer's individual crop insurance policy as depicted by the green box in the right-hand column. If an SCO policy is also purchased and there is also a loss at the county level, a indemnity from the SCO also would be paid (depicted by the blue box). Overall, the farmer incurs a loss of approximately 14% (white box at top), with the SCO indemnity reducing the "shallow loss" absorbed by the producer.

(SCO covers part of the deductible under the individual policy)

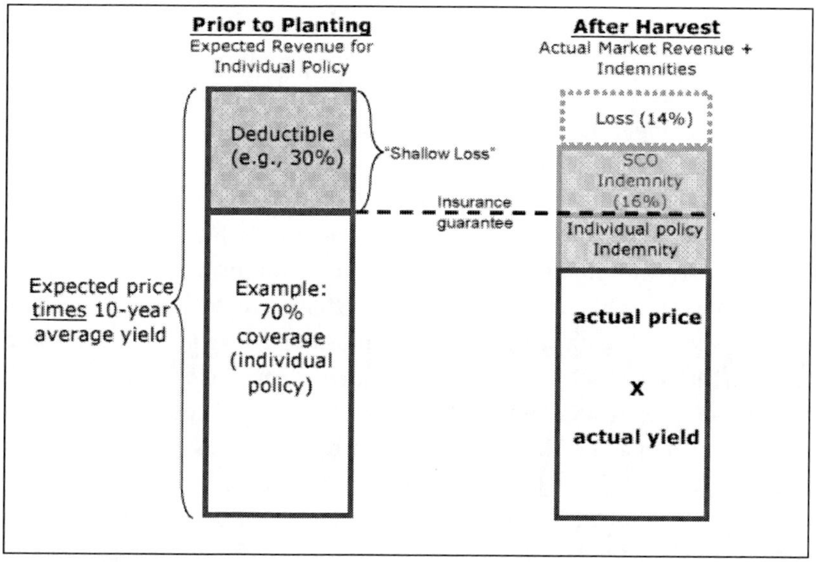

Source: CRS.

Notes: SCO indemnity (in blue box above) is triggered by a loss in county revenue (or yield if underlying individual policy is yield-based). Scenario assumes expected (and actual) revenue is the same at the individual farm and county level (SCO).

Figure 2. Supplemental Coverage Option (SCO) with a Crop Loss.

SCO is designed to serve as a "shallow loss" program for covered commodities enrolled by producers in Price Loss Coverage (PLC) under the farm commodity support program. A separate PLC payment would be made if the farm price for the crop is below a "reference price" set in statute. For crops enrolled in the alternative Agriculture Risk Coverage (ARC) program, SCO is not available because ARC is already designed to pay for "shallow losses."[11]

SCO policies are to be offered for crops that have sufficient data for policy development, and coverage is to begin no later than the 2015 crop year. USDA has announced plans for developing 2015 policies for corn, grain sorghum, rice, soybeans, winter wheat, spring wheat, and cotton.[12] The government subsidy as a share of the policy premium is 65%.

"Enterprise Units" and Yield Guarantees

Currently available policies are enhanced through a number of provisions beginning with the 2015 crop year. To provide better coverage for producers with both irrigated and nonirrigated crops, separate insurable "enterprise" units for each practice will be available (an enterprise unit is all land for a single crop in a county, regardless of the tenant/landlord structure). Separating the acreage can increase risk protection for producers because losses on dryland crops would no longer be offset by higher yields on irrigated acreage when the two are combined.

Another concern of producers in recent years has been the treatment of poor yields used to establish the insurance guarantee, which is based on 4 to 10 years of historical yields called actual production history (APH). Current law allows a "yield plug" if the producer's actual or appraised yield for any particularly year is less than 60% of the "transitional yield," generally based on the 10-year historical county average yield. The yield plug allows the replacement of a low actual yield in the APH with a yield equal to 60% of the applicable transitional yield. The 2014 farm bill enhances this provision by keeping the yield plug unchanged from current law (except in the case of native sod) but allowing producers to exclude without replacement any recorded or appraised yield from the APH calculation if the average crop yield in the county for any particular year is less than 50% of the 10-year county average.

Peanuts and Rice

The peanut and rice industries successfully argued for enhanced crop insurance options. The 2014 farm bill mandates a peanut revenue insurance product and rice margin insurance, with both to be made available for the 2015 crop year. For several years, rice producers have been interested in protecting against rising cost of inputs (e.g., fuel, fertilizer) as it affects their margin (income minus costs). For peanut producers, the revenue policy is to use the "Rotterdam price index" or other appropriate prices as determined by the Secretary. Setting the price guarantee is problematic for peanuts because the market is considered "thin," with only two peanut shellers reportedly buying over 80% of all peanuts from growers. No futures market exists for peanuts, and private contracts between producers and shellers reportedly account for most transactions, making it difficult to independently verify pricing needed to help set price parameters in the insurance policies.

Alfalfa and Industrial Crops

The 2014 farm bill also requires FCIC to enter into contracts to conduct research and development on modifications to insurance currently available for alfalfa through the "forage production" policy. Geographic coverage of the existing policy is limited, and supporters of the provision have said that loss coverage has been inadequate.

FCIC is also to research policies for crops currently not insurable, including biomass sorghum and sweet sorghum grown expressly for the purpose of producing a feedstock for renewable biofuel, renewable electricity, or biobased products.

Provisions for Specialty Crop Producers

Federal crop insurance is available for over 80 specialty crops (including fruit, tree nut, vegetable, and nursery crops), making the program the primary financial safety net for specialty crop producers. While additional policies have been introduced over the last 10 years, producer groups and some Members of Congress during the farm bill debate wanted to improve the safety net for specialty crops, in part since these crops are not eligible for farm commodity support programs.

Whole Farm Insurance

USDA is required to conduct more research on whole farm revenue insurance with higher coverage levels than currently available under the Adjusted Gross Revenue (AGR) and AGR-Lite policies which insure revenue of the entire farm rather than an individual crop.[13] In general, the AGR products are designed to protect producers with specialty crops and/or commodities not covered by individual policies. Historically, whole-farm insurance has seen limited participation, in part because the products are complex, the policies are available only in some parts of the country, and the maximum available coverage of 80% is considered too low for adequate risk protection.

FCIC has been working on a revised whole farm insurance plan that reportedly reflects provisions on whole farm insurance specified in the 2014 farm bill. The farm bill provisions include increasing available coverage from 80% to 85%, and a maximum liability of $1.5 million, up from $1 million for AGR-Lite. Also, eligible producers are to include direct-to-consumer marketers and producers who produce multiple agricultural commodities, including specialty crops, industrial crops, livestock, and aquaculture products. FCIC also may provide diversification-based additional coverage payment rates, premium discounts, or other enhanced benefits in recognition of the risk management benefits of crop and livestock diversification strategies for producers. FCIC can also expand coverage for the value of any packing, packaging, or any other similar on-farm activity that FCIC determines to be the minimum required in order to remove the commodity from the field.

Organic Prices for Insuring Crops

Current law requires FCIC to broaden coverage for organic crops. To reflect the higher product value and provide additional protection for producers, organic price elections have been made available for 16 crops as of early 2014. The 2014 farm bill extends the current practice by requiring FCIC to offer price elections by 2015 that reflect actual retail or wholesale prices of organic (not conventional) crops for all organic crops produced in compliance with standards issued by USDA under the Organic Foods Production Act of 1990.

"NAP" Enhancement

When crop insurance is not available, catastrophic coverage under the existing noninsured crop disaster assistance program (NAP) can be purchased from USDA's Farm Service Agency. NAP applicants pay an administrative fee (currently $250 per crop), and no premium is charged (like CAT crop insurance). In order to receive a NAP payment, a producer must experience at least a 50% crop loss caused by a natural disaster, or be prevented from planting more than 35% of intended crop acreage. For production losses in excess of the minimum, a producer receives 55% of the average market price for the commodity.

In order to expand coverage for specialty crops and others covered under NAP, the 2014 farm bill provides additional coverage at 50% to 65% of established yield and 100% of average market price. The farmer-paid premium for additional coverage is 5.25% times the product of the selected coverage level and value of production (acreage times yield times average market price). Also, the per-person payment limit is increased from $100,000 to $125,000. Separately, to assist producers with fruit crop losses in 2012, payments associated with additional coverage are made retroactively (minus premium fees) in counties declared a disaster due to freeze or frost.

Index-based Weather Insurance

FCIC is authorized to conduct two or more pilot programs (and approve subsequent policies) for index-based weather insurance. Index weather insurance protects against specific weather events and not actual losses. Priority is given to specialty crops (e.g., fruits and vegetables) and livestock commodities (including pasture, rangeland, and forage) that have had no available coverage or have low participation rates under existing coverage. The subsidy shall not exceed 60% of the estimated premium amount. Administrative and operating expenses are to be reimbursed as with other policies, but federal reinsurance, research and development costs, and other reimbursements or maintenance fees are not provided for these policies. Expenditures from the FCIC fund are limited to $12.5 million per year for FY2015-2018.

Policies may be sold by the approved insurance provider that submits the application as well as others who agree to pay maintenance fees to the submitting provider. Policies cannot be substantially similar to privately available hail insurance.

Food Safety Insurance Study

The 2014 farm bill requires FCIC to contract for a study on coverage for specialty crops that would indemnify producers for production or revenue losses related to food safety concerns such as government, retail, or national consumer group announcements of a health advisory, product removal, or recall related to a contamination concern. FCIC must submit a report to Congress within one year of enactment of the farm bill.

Studies for Animal Agriculture Insurance

Compared with the crop sector, the federal crop insurance program provides only limited coverage for the livestock industry. Relatively new or pilot programs protect livestock and dairy producers from loss of gross margin or price declines. Livestock producers can also insure against hay and forage losses through the Forage Production policy (see “Alfalfa and Industrial Crops” above) and the Pasture, Rangeland, and Forage program, which uses a rainfall index or vegetative index to determine loss.

The 2014 farm bill directs FCIC to study a variety of topics that could lead to additional insurance policies for animal agriculture. FCIC is required to enter into contracts to conduct research and development on policies for the margin between the market value of catfish and input costs and poultry business interruption insurance for poultry growers, including losses due to bankruptcy of an integrator (owner-processor). FCIC is also required to contract for studies on insuring swine producers for a catastrophic event and insuring poultry producers for a catastrophic event.

Conservation Provisions

As directed in the conservation title (II) of the 2014 farm bill, crop insurance premium subsidies are available only if producers are in compliance with wetland conservation requirements and conservation requirements for highly erodible land. USDA expects most producers will be unaffected because the same requirement has been in place for years to maintain eligibility for farm program and other USDA benefits.

Also, to limit the incentive to convert native sod to cropland, a separate provision in the crop insurance title affects producers purchasing policies for crop insurance or noninsured crop disaster assistance program (NAP). For the first four years of planting on native sod acreage in Iowa, Minnesota, Montana, Nebraska, North Dakota, and South Dakota, farmers will pay more for the risk coverage through reduced crop insurance subsidies or higher NAP fees, and the yield guarantee is reduced compared to other cropland. For details, see *Table A-1*.

Provisions for Beginning Farmers

To help develop the next generation of producers, the 2014 farm bill makes several changes to benefit beginning farmers or ranchers with less than five years of experience. For example, to reduce the cost of purchasing crop insurance for beginning farmers or ranchers, the $300 fee for purchasing catastrophic (CAT) coverage is waived. Also, the premium subsidy schedule for additional coverage is increased by 10 percentage points.

To boost the yield guarantee for beginning farmers, the calculation can now use yields recorded by prior producers on the acreage, which might be higher than the alternative when historical data are not available (i.e., 65% of the transitional yield based on county average yields). When historical data are available to establish the producer's actual production history, beginning farmers can replace low yields with a yield equal to 80% of the transitional yield.

Similar benefits are provided under the noninsured crop disaster assistance program (NAP), which provides catastrophic coverage for uninsurable crops. The provision extends the fee waiver for basic NAP coverage to beginning farmers and socially disadvantaged farmers. Premium for additional NAP coverage is reduced by 50% for limited resource, beginning, and socially disadvantaged farmers.[14]

"Budget Neutral" for the Next Standard Reinsurance Agreement

As authorized by the 2008 farm bill, the Federal Crop Insurance Corporation (FCIC) negotiated with private companies to revise the Standard Reinsurance Agreement (SRA) to save federal money and improve program delivery in underserved areas. The SRA, in place since 2011, governs the terms under which the government pays participating insurance companies to sell and service policies and shares underwriting gains or losses with them. The changes made in 2011 put a cap on administrative and operating (A&O) costs and limited agent commissions, measures opposed by the crop insurance companies. Some but not all of the estimated $6 billion in budget savings over 10 years was reinvested back into crop insurance, including expansion of the Pasture, Rangeland, and Forage crop insurance program. FCIC may renegotiate the SRA once every five years.

To ensure that insurance companies are not adversely affected by changes in the next SRA, the 2014 farm bill requires that any revised SRA is budget neutral with respect to estimates of future underwriting gains for the private companies, and the estimated total A&O reimbursements cannot be less than the amounts that would have been provided under the previous SRA. The Manager's Report states their intent is that a renegotiated SRA should not be used as a means of achieving further cuts in the federal crop insurance program. During the farm bill debate, some Members of Congress argued that such cuts, if any, should be made by Congress so it could claim the budget savings towards either deficit reduction or to offset the cost of any new legislative initiative.

Premium Subsidies

Unlike farm commodity programs, the federal crop insurance program does not have an income limit test for program eligibility or premium subsidy limits. The topic was widely discussed in Congress during the farm bill debate, particularly in 2012 and 2013.

A controversial item not included in P.L. 113-79 was the reduction of premium subsidies for high income farmers, a provision that was included in the Senate bill but not the House bill. In the 2012 farm bill passed by the Senate in the 112th Congress, an amendment was adopted during floor debate to reduce crop insurance premium subsidies by 15 percentage points for producers with average adjusted gross income greater than $750,000. In 2013, the Senate Agriculture Committee-reported version of S. 954 did not include the provision, but an amendment to S. 954 requiring the subsidy reduction was adopted on the Senate floor in June 2013 by a vote of 59-33. A House amendment to limit crop insurance premium subsidies failed during floor debate in June 2013.[15]

ESTIMATED COST OF THE CROP INSURANCE TITLE

Prior to enactment of the 2014 farm bill, projected baseline expenditures for the federal crop insurance program were estimated at $84.1 billion over 10 years, according to the Congressional Budget Office. The enacted 2014 farm bill (P.L. 113-79) increased expected outlays for crop insurance relative to this 10-year baseline level by an additional $5.7 billion (*Table 1*).

Table 1. Cost of Provisions in the Crop Insurance Title of the 2014 Farm Bill (in millions of dollars)

Description	5 years: FY2014-FY2018	10 years: FY2014-FY2023
CBO baseline, May 2013, Crop Insurance	39,592	84,105
CBO score of changes in Title XI (Crop Insurance) of the 2014 farm bill		
Provisions with net savings:		
Premium amounts for catastrophic (CAT) crop insurance	-153	-426
Crop production on native sod	-34	-114
Participation effects of commodity programs[a]	-240	-464
Provisions with net additional costs:		
Supplemental Coverage Option (SCO)	544	1,716
Crop margin coverage	15	40
Enterprise units for irrigated and nonirrigated crops	188	533
Adjustment in actual producer history (APH) yields	120	357
Coverage level by practice	60	168
Beginning farmer and rancher provisions	84	261
Stacked Income Protection (STAX) for cotton	1,054	3,288
Peanut revenue crop insurance	44	119
Implementation	55	70
Crop insurance fraud	36	81
Research and development priorities	16	36
Crop Insurance for organic crops	3	8
Index-based weather insurance	37	50
Subtotal: CBO Score of 2014 Farm Bill changes, Title XI	1,828	5,722
CBO Estimate of Total Cost of Crop Insurance	41,420	89,827

Source: CBO baseline and score of the conference agreement of H.R. 2642, the Agricultural Act of 2014, as reported on January 27, 2014.

Notes: Changes to the noninsured crop assistance program (NAP) in Title XII are estimated to increase outlays by $159 million during 2014-2018 and $226 million during 2014-2023.

[a] Producers are expected to purchase less crop insurance (which reduces federal costs) when participating in the Agricultural Risk Coverage (ARC) program authorized in Title I.

The largest cost items are the Stacked Income Protection (STAX) for cotton, estimated at $3.3 billion over 10 years, and the Supplemental Coverage Option (SCO), estimated at $1.7 billion over 10 years. Several general enhancements involve expanded coverage for irrigated crops and revising yield history for setting yield guarantees. The combined cost of these upgrades is more than $1 billion over 10 years.

The largest cost savings item for Title XI relates to the interaction between crop insurance and farm programs authorized in Title I. The Agricultural Risk Coverage (ARC) program is designed to cover some losses that crop insurance might otherwise cover. Therefore, producers who enroll their crop in ARC might purchase reduced coverage levels for crop insurance, which would reduce federal expenditures on total premium subsidies and administrative and operating costs.

APPENDIX. CROP INSURANCE PROVISIONS IN THE ENACTED 2014 FARM BILL

Table A-1. Crop Insurance Provisions in the Enacted 2014 Farm Bill Compared with Previous Law

Previous Law/Policy	2014 Farm Bill (P.L. 113-79)
Information Sharing and Publication of Violations	
USDA, an approved insurance provider and its employees and contractors, and any other person may not disclose to the public information furnished by a producer unless it has been aggregated to avoid disclosure of an individual's information. *[7 U.S.C. 1502(c)]*	Adds provision that, if authorized by a producer, USDA's Farm Service Agency is to provide to an insurance agent or approved insurance provider any information or maps that may assist the agent or provider insuring the producer. *[Sec. 11001]*
Adjustments to producer premiums are prohibited as an inducement to purchase crop insurance, with few exceptions. *[7 U.S.C. 1508(a)(9)]*	To deter potential violators, the Federal Crop Insurance Corporation (FCIC) is required to publish in detail (but without disclosing identities) any violations of the existing prohibition on adjustments to premiums, including sanctions imposed. *[Sec. 11002]*
Supplemental Coverage Option (SCO)	
No comparable provision.	Makes available to crop producers a policy called Supplemental Coverage Option (SCO) to cover part of the deductible under the producer's underlying policy. SCO is an area-wide (e.g., county) yield or revenue loss policy, whereby an indemnity is paid on area losses not more than the deductible

Previous Law/Policy	2014 Farm Bill (P.L. 113-79)
	level (e.g., 25%) selected by the producer for the underlying individual policy. Coverage is triggered by losses greater than 14%, and policy coverage cannot exceed the difference between 86% and the coverage level selected by the producer for the underlying policy. Acres covered by Agriculture Risk Coverage (ARC) or STAX (see below) are not eligible for SCO. SCO policies are to be made available for all crops if sufficient data are available. Premium subsidized at 65%. Coverage to begin no later than the 2015 crop year. *[Sec. 11003]* A crop margin coverage option is available as a single policy or in combination with a yield or revenue loss policy. *[Sec. 11004]*
Catastrophic Yield Policies (CAT)	
Catastrophic yield policies (CAT) are available for yield losses greater than 50%. Premium is fully subsidized, and producer pays an administrative fee of $300 per crop per county. Participating crop insurance companies are reimbursed for selling and servicing the policies based on the premium amount. *[7 U.S.C. 1508(d)(2)]*	CAT remains fully subsidized, and reimbursements to private insurance companies remain tied to the calculated premium. To reduce government costs of reimbursement, the calculated premium is reduced by the percentage equal to the difference between the average loss ratio (premiums divided by indemnities times 100) for the crop and 100%, plus a reasonable reserve as determined by FCIC. *[Sec. 11005]* In Title XII—Miscellaneous: Prohibits CAT coverage on crops and grasses used for grazing. *[Sec. 12305(b)]*
Enterprise and Whole Farm Units	
Crops are insured based on geographic units defined in the insurance policy. The basic unit covers land in one county with the same tenant/landlord. An optional unit is a basic unit divided into smaller units by township section. An enterprise unit covers all land of a single crop in a county for a producer, regardless of tenant/landlord structure. A whole farm unit covers more than one crop. For a policy with an enterprise or whole farm unit paragraph, *on a pilot basis,* the	The subsidy for enterprise and whole farm units is made permanent (previously apilot basis). *[Sec. 11006]* Beginning with the 2015 crop year, separate enterprise units will be available for irrigated and nonirrigated acreages of crops. *[Sec. 11007]*

Table A-1. (Continued)

Previous Law/Policy	2014 Farm Bill (P.L. 113-79)
percentage of the premium paid by the government shall provide the same dollar amount of premium subsidy per acre as for other units, up to 80%. *[7 U.S.C. 1508(e)(5)]*	
Data Collection for Yield Guarantees; Yield Adjustments	
FCIC bases policy guarantees on a producer's actual production history (APH) for the crop, or on county yields for area-wide policies. The APH is based on producer yields for the prior 4 to 10 years. *[7 U.S.C. 1508(g)(2)]*	Specifically directs FCIC to use county data collected by USDA's Risk Management Agency and/or National Agricultural Statistics Service. If such data are not available, it may use other data considered appropriate by the Secretary of Agriculture. *[Sec.11008]*
If, for one or more of the crop years used to establish the producer's actual production history (APH) of an agricultural commodity, the producer's recorded or appraised yield of the commodity was less than 60% of the applicable transitional yield (based on 10-year historical county average yield), FCIC can at the election of the producer exclude the recorded or appraised yield and replace it with a yield equal to 60% of the applicable transitional yield. Concept is known as yield substitution with a "yield plug." *[7 U.S.C. 1508(g)(4)(B)]*	Yield plug remains unchanged from current law but producers may elect to exclude any recorded or appraised yield from the APH calculation if the crop yield in the county is less than 50% of the 10-year county average. Separate determinations are made for irrigated and nonirrigated acreage. Producers in contiguous (adjacent) counties can do the same. *[Sec. 11009]*
Policy Research Development, Review, Approval, and Cost Reimbursement	
An approved insurance provider, a college or university, a cooperative or trade association, or others may prepare for submission or propose to FCIC crop insurance policies and provisions of policies. *[7 U.S.C. 1508(h)(1)]* Under sections 522 and 523 of the Federal Crop Insurance Act, FCIC may enter into contracts to carry out research and development for new crop insurance policies (but may not conduct research itself). FCIC shall establish as one of the highest research priorities the development of a pasture, range, and forage program. It shall provide a	ddsrequirement that FCIC must review and submit to the FCIC Board any policy developed under section 522(c) or pilot program developed under section 523 if FCIC determines that it will likely result in (i) a viable and marketable policy, (ii) would provide crop insurance coverage in a significantly improved form, and (iii) adequately protects the interests of producers. Also, the Board shall review and approve for sale a new policy if the Board determines: (i) the interests of producers are adequately protected, (ii) the proposed policy will: (I)

Previous Law/Policy	2014 Farm Bill (P.L. 113-79)
payment to an applicant for research and development costs. *[7 U.S.C. 1522]*	provide a new kind of coverage that is likely to be viable and marketable; (II) provide crop insurance coverage in a manner that addresses a clear and identifiable flaw or problem in an existing policy; or (III) provide a new kind of coverage for a commodity that previously had no available crop insurance, or has demonstrated a low level of participation or coverage level under existing coverage; and (iii) the proposed policy will not have a significant adverse impact on the crop insurance delivery system. The Board is to give first priority to new policies that address underserved commodities (limited or no available coverage), and then to existing policies for which there is inadequate coverage or there exists low levels of participation. Requires by the 2015 crop year a revenue policy for peanut producers and a margin coverage policy for rice producers. *[Sec. 11010(a)]*
The Board may approve up to 50% of the projected total research and development costs to be paid in advance to an applicant if it determines that: (i) the concept will likely result in a viable and marketable policy consistent with section 1508(h) of this title; (ii) in the sole opinion of the Board, the concept would provide crop insurance coverage-(I) in a significantly improved form; (II) to a crop or region not traditionally served by the federal crop insurance program; or (III) in a form that addresses a recognized flaw or problem in the program; (iii) the applicant agrees to provide such reports as FCIC determines are necessary to monitor the development effort; (iv) the proposed budget and timetable are reasonable; and (v) the concept proposal meets any other requirements that the Board determines appropriate. *[7 U.S.C. 1522(b)(2)]*	Same as current law and authorizes Board to waive the 50% limitation and approve an additional 25% advance payment if the intended policy will provide coverage for a region or crop that is underserved by the federal crop insurance program, including specialty crops, and the submitter is making satisfactory progress towards developing a viable and marketable policy. *[Sec. 11010(b)]*

Table A-1. (Continued)

Previous Law/Policy	2014 Farm Bill (P.L. 113-79)
A private sector entity can propose an insurance plan to be added to the FCIC portfolio of products. A process must be established to review and approve products. *[7 U.S.C. 1508(h)(4)]*	As part of the submission process for policies involving fruits and vegetables, tree nuts, dried fruits, and horticulture and nursery crops (including floriculture), the applicant must consult with producer groups potentially affected. Any submission must contain a summary of these findings. FCIC shall determine if the policy will create adverse market distortions. *[Sec. 11011]*
Standard Reinsurance Agreement and Risk-Sharing	
The Standard Reinsurance Agreement (SRA) between FCIC and private companies defines expense reimbursements and risk-sharing by the government, including the terms under which the government provides subsidies and reinsurance (i.e., insurance for insurance companies) on eligible crop insurance contracts sold or reinsured by insurance companies. FCIC may renegotiate the SRA once every 5 years. *[7 U.S.C. 1508(k)(8)]*	Any renegotiated SRA is to be budget neutral with respect to underwriting gains. Also, estimated reimbursement for administrative and operating (A&O) costs cannot be less than the amounts under the immediately preceding SRA if it were extended. Any budget savings from a renegotiated SRA shall be used to increase underwriting gains or A&O reimbursements. *[Sec. 11012]*
Corn with Low Test	
Under an insurance policy, if an agricultural commodity does not meet established quality standards, actual production (used for determining the indemnity) is reduced accordingly. *[7 U.S.C. 1508(m)]*	FCIC shall establish procedures to allow insured producers not more than 120 days to settle claims involving corn that is determined to have low test weight. FCIC is to implement this provision on a regional basis based on market conditions and the interests of producers. Authority for this provision terminates 5 years after implementation. *[Sec. 11013]*
Crop Production on Native Sod ("Sod Saver") and Conservation Compliance Sod Saver: Subject to a geographic condition below, native sod planted to an insurable crop (over 5 acres) is ineligible for crop insurance and the noninsured crop disaster assistance program (NAP) for the first 5 years of planting. May apply to virgin prairie converted to cropland only in the Prairie Pothole National Priority Area, if elected by	During the first 4 years of planting, crop insurance and NAP benefits are reduced on native sod acreage in Minnesota, Iowa, North Dakota, South Dakota, Montana, and Nebraska. Provisions include: (1) a reduction in the crop insurance premium subsidy by 50 percentage points, and NAP fee is doubled; (2) annual data for APH are equal to 65% of the transitional yield for all four years rather than the higher, variable

Previous Law/Policy	2014 Farm Bill (P.L. 113-79)
the state. *[7 U.S.C. 1508(o)]* and *[7 U.S.C. 7333(a)(4)]* To complete the actual production history (APH) database used for calculating the yield guarantee, a farmer can use a variable percentage of the transitional yield (Tyield), depending on the number of years of actual history: 1 year = 80%, 2 years =90%, 3 years =100%. *[p. 254 of the 2014 Crop Insurance Handbook, FCIC18010]* Yield substitutes are allowed. *[See above: 7 U.S.C. 1508(g)(4)(B)]*	percentage applicable for other cropland; and (3) for crop insurance, yield substitutes are not allowed; that is, low farm yields must be used in the APH rather than replacing them with potentially higher T-yields. (On other cropland, producers can substitute 60% of the T-yield for any actual yield below 60% of the T-yield). USDA is required to submit an annual report to Congress that describes cropland acreage in each applicable county and state, and the change in cropland acreage from the preceding year, beginning with calendar year 2000. *[Sec. 11014]*
Conservation Compliance: In exchange for certain USDA program benefits, including commodity support programs, conservation programs, disaster payments, and operating loans, a producer agrees to maintain a minimum level of conservation on highly erodible land. Highly erodible land can be considered eligible for program benefits if the land user agrees to cultivate the land using an approved conservation plan or qualifies for an exemption. *[16 U.S.C. 3811 et seq.]*	In Title II—Conservation: Adds the federally funded portion of crop insurance premiums to the list of program benefits that could be lost if a producer is found to produce an agricultural commodity on certain converted wetlands or highly erodible land without an approved conservation plan or qualifying exemption. Violation resulting in ineligibility for crop insurance subsidy payments applies to reinsurance years subsequent to the date of the final determination of a violation (including all appeals). *[Sec. 2611(a)]*
Coverage Levels by Practice	
No comparable provision.	Beginning with the 2015 crop year, a producer who grows a crop on both dry land and irrigated land may elect a different coverage level for each production practice. *[Sec. 11015]*
Provisions for Beginning Farmers and Ranchers	
For catastrophic risk protection (CAT), producers pay an administrative fee of $300 per crop per county. *[7 U.S.C. 1508(b)(5)(A)]* The fee is waived for limited resource farmers (defined by USDA as those who have farm sales not more than $172,800 and household income at or below the national poverty level for a family of four). *[7 U.S.C. 1508(b)(5)(E)]* Premium subsidies	"Beginning farmer or rancher' means a farmer or rancher who has not actively operated and managed a farm or ranch with a bona fide insurable interest in a crop or livestock as an owner-operator, landlord, tenant, or sharecropper for more than 5 crop years, The following is provided for beginning farmers or ranchers: (1) waiver of CAT fees, (2) premium assistance that is 10

Table A-1. (Continued)

Previous Law/Policy	2014 Farm Bill (P.L. 113-79)
for buy-up coverage (above CAT) depend on level of coverage. *[7 U.S.C. 1508(e)]* For producers without historical yield data, the assigned yield in yield coverage plans is not less than 65% of the transitional yield of the producer or as determined by FCIC. *[7 U.S.C. 1508(g)(2)(B)]* When FCIC uses the actual production records of the producer to establish the producer's actual production history, an individual year may be excluded from the yield history if the appraised yield is less than 60% of the transitional yield, and the excluded yield can be replaced with a yield equal to 60% of the transitional yield. *[7 U.S.C. 1508(g)(4)(B)(ii)]*	percentage points greater than general subsidy schedule, (3) in the absence of historical data, an assigned yield that can be based on the crop yields recorded by prior producers on the acreage, and (4) excluded yields can be replaced with a yield equal to 80% of the transitional yield. *[Sec. 11016]*
New Policies: Stacked Income Protection Plan (STAX) for Producers of Upland Cotton and Peanut Revenue Crop Insurance	
No comparable provision.	Beginning with the 2015 crop, the FCIC shall make available to producers of upland cotton the Stacked Income Protection Plan (STAX), which is a revenue-based, areawide policy that may be purchased as a stand-alone policy or purchased in addition to any other individual or area policy. Indemnifies losses in county revenue of greater than 10% of expected revenue but not more than the deductible level (e.g., 25%) selected by the producer for the underlying individual policy (or not more than 30% used as stand-alone policy). Coverage is based on the expected price used for existing area-wide policies and the higher of expected county yields established for existing area-wide policies or the 5-year Olympic average county yield (Olympic average excludes the high and low years), using data from USDA's Risk Management Agency and/or National Agricultural Statistics Service or other data as considered appropriate by the Secretary). Indemnities are paid based on the amount that the actual county revenue falls

Previous Law/Policy	2014 Farm Bill (P.L. 113-79)
	short of the expected county revenue, as applied to the individual coverage of the producer. For individual producers, indemnities for STAX and other policies cannot overlap. The premium subsidy is 80% plus the amount for A&O. The calculated premium covers: (1) anticipated losses and a reasonable reserve, and (2) an amount for administrative and operating expenses. Policies are to be offered in all producing counties at the county level, or on the basis of a larger geographic area if necessary. Separate coverage levels are available for irrigated and nonirrigated practices. A factor of not more than 120% is available to increase protection per acre *[Sec. 11017]* Cotton is not a covered commodity eligible for Price Loss Coverage (PLC) or Agriculture Risk Coverage (ARC) in Title I of the 2014 farm bill. *[Sec. 1111(6)]*
No comparable provision.	Beginning with the 2015 crop year, the FCIC shall make available a revenue policy for peanut producers and use the Rotterdam price index or other appropriate prices as determined by the Secretary. The effective price may be adjusted to correct distortions, but the adjustment must be done in an open and transparent manner and a report must be submitted to Congress describing the reasons for the adjustment. *[Sec. 11018] The* approval of a peanut revenue policy is to be made a priority for FCIC. *[Sec. 11010(a)]*
Correcting Errors	
To improve program compliance and integrity, FCIC shall work with approved insurance providers to address program compliance and integrity issues. *[7 U.S.C. 1515(a)(2)]* Inaccurate information on an insurance application can result in noncompliance, which voids the policy and may result in civil fines and program disqualification for up to 5 years. *[7 U.S.C.*	FCIC shall establish procedures that allow an agent and approved insurance provider to correct (within a reasonable amount of time) errors in information that is provided by a producer to ensure that the eligibility (and other) information is correct and consistent with information reported by the producer for other USDA programs. Additional provisions allow for corrections of data

Table A-1. (Continued)

Previous Law/Policy	2014 Farm Bill (P.L. 113-79)
1515(h)] The FCIC and USDA's Farm Service Agency shall reconcile producer-derived information on at least an annual basis in order to identify and address any discrepancies. *[7 U.S.C. 1515(c)]*	issued by the Farm Service Agency or electronic transmission errors made by an agent, approved insurance provider, or USDA agencies. Correction may only be made if they do not allow the producer to: (1) avoid ineligibility requirements for insurance or obtain a disproportionate benefit; (2) obtain and enhance an insurance guarantee or indemnity if a cause of loss exists or has occurred before any correction has been made, or avoid premium owed if no loss is likely to occur; or (3) avoid an obligation or requirement under any federal or state law. Any corrections made within a reasonable amount of time shall not be subject to late filing fees. Also, provides authority to allow a producer to purchase crop insurance after the sales closing date under certain conditions. *[Sec. 11019]*
Implementation and Fraud Detection	
USDA is to ensure that new hardware and software for administering the program are compatible with that already used by USDA agencies in order to maximize data sharing needed for proper program delivery. *[7 U.S.C. 1515(j)]* Funding is provided from the insurance fund: $15 million for each of FY2008 through FY2010 and not more than $9 million in FY2011. *[7 U.S.C. 1515(k]*	USDA shall develop and implement an Acreage Crop Reporting Streamlining Initiative (ACRSI) project to allow producers to report acreage and other information directly to USDA. FCIC may use up to $14 million in FY2014 and $9 million per year for FY2015 through FY2018 from the insurance fund. An additional $5 million per year is available for each of FY2015-2018 if the ACRSI project is substantially completed by September 30, 2015. USDA shall notify Congress on the status of the project no later than July 1, 2015. *[Sec. 11020]*
FCIC may use up to $3.5 million of the insurance fund to pay for costs associated with implementing plans of insurance and for review of policies. *[7 U.S.C. 1516(b)(2)]*	Adds authority to use up to $9 million per year of the insurance fund to pay for costs associated with maintaining program integrity and compliance activities and to assist in maintaining program actuarial soundness and financial integrity. *[Sec. 11021]*
Research and Development Priorities	

Previous Law/Policy	2014 Farm Bill (P.L. 113-79)
FCIC may enter into contracts to carry out research and development for new crop insurance policies but may not conduct research itself. FCIC shall establish as one of the highest research priorities the development of a pasture, range, and forage program. *[7 U.S.C. 1522(c)]*	In addition to contracting, allows FCIC to conduct research and development activities to maintain or improve existing policies or develop new policies. *[Sec. 11022(a)(1-3)]* Replaces the priority on pasture, range, and forage program with policies that increase participation by producers of underserved agricultural commodities, including sweet sorghum, biomass sorghum, rice, peanuts, sugarcane, alfalfa, pennycress, dedicated energy crops, and specialty crops. *[Sec. 11022(a)(5)]* Requires FCIC to enter into contracts to conduct research and development on policies for: (1) the margin between the market value of catfish and input costs; (2) biomass sorghum and sweet sorghum grown expressly for the purpose of producing a feedstock for renewable biofuel, renewable electricity, or biobased products; (3) whole farm insurance (see below); (4) poultry business interruptions insurance for poultry growers, including losses due to bankruptcy of an integrator (ownerprocessor), with research contract entered within 180 days of enactment of the farm bill and a summary report submitted to Congress within 1 year of enactment; and (5) alfalfa crop insurance, with a summary report submitted to Congress within 1 year of enactment of the farm bill. *[Sec. 11022(a)(7)]* Requires FCIC to contract for studies on: (1) insuring swine producers for a catastrophic event, (2) insuring poultry producers for a catastrophic event, (3) providing production or revenue loss coverage for specialty crops related to food safety and contaminations issues, including public announcements. FCIC must submit reports on each to Congress within 1 year of enactment of the farm bill. *[Sec. 11022(a)(7)]*
Adjusted Gross Revenue (AGR) and AGR-Lite policies insure revenue of the entire farm rather than an individual crop. Both use	Unless FCIC approves an enhanced whole farm insurance plan by 2016, FCIC shall conduct activities or enter into contracts to

Table A-1. (Continued)

Previous Law/Policy	2014 Farm Bill (P.L. 113-79)
a producer's five-year historical farm average revenue as reported on the Internal Revenue Service (IRS) tax return form (Schedule F or equivalent forms). Coverage levels range from 65% to 80% of historical revenue, and maximum liability is $6.5 million for AGR and $1million for AGR-Lite. *[7 U.S.C. 1523]*	carry out research and development to develop an enhanced version of the whole farm risk management insurance plan. Available coverage is increased from 80% to 85%, and maximum liability is $1.5 million (up from $1 million for AGR-Lite). Eligible producers include direct-toconsumer marketers and producers who produce multiple agricultural commodities, including specialty crops, industrial crops, livestock, and aquaculture products. The FCIC may provide diversification-based additional coverage payment rates, premium discounts, or other enhanced benefits in recognition of the risk management benefits of crop and livestock diversification strategies for producers. The FCIC also may include coverage for the value of any packing, packaging, or any other similar on-farm activity that FCIC determines to be the minimum required in order to remove the commodity from the field. *[Sec. 11022(a)(7)]*
Miscellaneous	
Organic policies: Requires FCIC to improve coverage for organic crops. *[U.S.C. 1522(c)(10)]* As of early 2014, USDA offered organic price elections for 16 crops, which increases the insurable value for organic producers.	By 2015, requires FCIC to offer price elections that reflect actual retail or wholesale prices of organic (not conventional) crops. Applies to all organic crops produced in compliance with standards issued by USDA under the Organic Foods Production Act of 1990. FCIC must submit an annual report to Congress on crop insurance for organic crops. *[Sec. 11023]*
Partnerships for risk management development and implementation: FCIC is authorized to enter into partnerships with public and private entities for the purpose of increasing the availability of loss mitigation, financial, and other risk management tools for producers, with a priority given to risk management tools for	Revises the purpose and objective of partnerships to also include improving analysis tools and technology regarding compliance or identifying and using innovative compliance strategies. *[Sec. 11024]* Adds "farm financial benchmarking" to the list of partnership objectives. The term is

Previous Law/Policy	2014 Farm Bill (P.L. 113-79)
producers of agricultural commodities covered by the noninsured crop assistance program (NAP), specialty crops, and underserved agricultural commodities. *[U.S.C. 1522(d)]*	defined as the process of comparing the performance of an agricultural enterprise against the performance of other similar enterprises through the use of comparable and reliable data, in order to identify business management strengths, weaknesses, and steps necessary to improve business profitability. *[Sec. 11027]*
Pilot programs: FCIC may conduct a pilot program submitted to and approved by the Board to evaluate whether a proposal or new risk management tool is suitable for the marketplace and addresses the needs of producers. After the completion of pilot program, FCIC shall submit to Congress a report on its operation and include recommendations on implementing the program on a national basis. *[7 U.S.C. 1523(a)]* FCIC shall not conduct any pilot program that provides insurance protection against a risk if a policy is generally available from private companies. *[7 U.S.C. 1523(a)(2)]*	Eliminates the requirement that FCIC evaluate pilot programs and submit a report to Congress. *[Sec. 11025]* FCIC is authorized to conduct two or more pilot programs to provide producers of underserved specialty crops and livestock commodities (including pasture, rangeland, and forage) with index-based weather insurance. The FCIC Board shall approve two or more proposed policies, if certain conditions are met, including experience and financial requirements of the approved provider. Priority is given to new kinds of coverage for specialty crops and livestock that previously had no available crop insurance or have low participation under existing coverage. The subsidy shall not exceed 60% of the estimated premium amount. Administrative and operating expenses are to be reimbursed, but federal reinsurance, research and development costs, and other reimbursements or maintenance fees are not provided for these policies. Policies may be sold only by the approved provider that submits the application; others may also sell them if maintenance fees are paid to the provider who submitted the proposal. The FCIC must develop and publish procedures that (1) require each approved insurance provider to report sales, acreage, and claim data to allow FCIC to evaluate sales and performance; and (2) ensure that the products do not have a significant adverse impact on the crop insurance delivery system, are in the best interests of producers, and do not result in a

Table A-1. (Continued)

Previous Law/Policy	2014 Farm Bill (P.L. 113-79)
	reduction of program integrity. Policies cannot be substantially similar to privately available hail insurance. Mandatory funding from FCIC fund is limited to $12.5 million per year for FY2015-2018. *[Sec. 11026]*
Education and risk management assistance: The Secretary, acting through the National Institute of Food and Agriculture, shall establish a program under which competitive grants are made to qualified public and private entities (including land grant colleges, cooperative extension services, and colleges or universities) for the purpose of educating agricultural producers about the full range of risk management activities, including futures, options, agricultural trade options, crop insurance, cash forward contracting, debt reduction, production diversification, farm resources risk reduction, and other risk management strategies. *[7 U.S.C. 1524(a)(3)(A)]*	Adds farm financial benchmarking to the list of risk management activities. *[Sec. 11027]*
No comparable provision.	Various technical amendments, including a provision that requires notice to Congress if the Standard Reinsurance Agreement is renegotiated. *[Sec. 11028]*
Noninsured Crop Disaster Assistance Program (NAP)	
The Noninsured Crop Disaster Assistance Program (NAP) has permanent authority under Section 196 of the Federal Agriculture Improvement and Reform Act of 1996, and receives such sums as necessary in mandatory funding. Growers of crops not insurable under the crop insurance program are eligible for NAP. A payment is made to an eligible producer whose actual production is less than 50% of the established (historical) yield for the crop. The payment rate is 55% of the average market price. Producers pay a fee of $250 per crop per county, or $750 per producer per county, not	In Title XII—Miscellaneous: Makes available for crop years 2015-2018 additional coverage under NAP at 50% to 65% of established yield and 100% of average market price. Premium for additional coverage is 5.25% times the product of the selected coverage level and value of production (acreage times yield times average market price). The maximum premium is 5.25% times the payment limit ($125,000). Extends fee waiver for basic NAP coverage to beginning and socially disadvantaged farmers. Premium for additional NAP

Previous Law/Policy	2014 Farm Bill (P.L. 113-79)
to exceed $1,875 per producer. The fee is waived for a limited resource farmer. The Farm Service Agency administers the program. *[7 USC 7333]*	coverage is reduced by 50% for limited resource, beginning, and socially disadvantaged farmers. For producers with fruit crop losses in 2012, payments associated with additional coverage are made retroactively (minus premium fees) in counties declared a disaster due to freeze or frost. Maintains industrial crops as eligible for NAP but specifies that industrial crops include those grown expressly for the purpose of producing a feedstock for renewable biofuel, renewable electricity, or biobased products. Specifically adds sweet sorghum and biomass sorghum to list of eligible crops for NAP. Crops and grasses for grazing are not eligible for additional coverage but remain eligible for catastrophic coverage. *[Sec. 12305(a)]*
The total amount of payments received per person for any crop year may not exceed $100,000. *[7 USC 7333(i)(2)]*	Payment limit is increased to $125,000. *[Sec. 12305(a)(2)]*

Source: CRS.

End Notes

[1] Additional background on the federal crop insurance program is available in CRS Report R40532, Federal Crop Insurance: Background.

[2] Randall A. Kramer, "Federal Crop Insurance 1938-1982," Agricultural History, vol. 57, no. 2 (April 1983), pp. 181- 200.

[3] An example of hail or fire insurance is https://www.rainhail.com/pdf_files/MKTG/MKTG_4000.pdf. Examples of other single peril coverage include (1) insurance for specific weather variables such as low temperature offered by Total Weather Insurance, http://climate.com/products/total-weather-insurance/; and (2) riders on federal policies to increase crop price protection contained in the Hudson Insurance Price Flex contract, http://www.hudsoncrop.com/index.php?option=com_content&view=article&id=51&Itemid=70.

[4] Vincent H. Smith and Barry K. Goodwin, "Private and Public Roles in Providing Agricultural Insurance in the United States," in Public Insurance and Private Markets, ed. Jeffrey R. Brown (Washington, DC: AEI Press, 2010), p. 184.

[5] Joseph W. Glauber, "Crop Insurance Reconsidered," Amer. J. Agr. Econ., vol. 86, no. 5 (2004), pp. 1179-1195.

[6] Producers who grow a crop not covered by crop insurance can purchase coverage through the Noninsured Crop Disaster Assistance Program (NAP). For more information, see CRS Report RS21212, Agricultural Disaster Assistance.

[7] This transfer of risk is accomplished through a set of reinsurance funds maintained by FCIC. The assigned risk fund, for example, is used by companies for policies believed to be high-risk because it provides the most loss protection to insurance companies through "stop-loss" coverage that reinsures against state-level disasters.

[8] As part of the transition, farm payments are made for upland cotton for the 2014 crop year, and for 2015 if STAX is not available. Payment acres in 2014 equal 60% of 2013 cotton base acres and 36.5% of 2013 cotton base acres in 2015. For more information on PLC and ARC, see CRS Report R43448, Farm Commodity Provisions in the 2014 Farm Bill (P.L. 113-79). For information on the cotton trade case, see CRS Report R43336, Status of the WTO BrazilU.S. Cotton Case.

[9] The revenue guarantee is the producer's selected coverage level times the expected per-acre revenue prior to planting (expected yield times expected price). The expected county yield is the higher of either the historical yield used for existing area-wide policies or the five-year county area average yield, excluding the high and low years, using data from USDA's Risk Management Agency and/or National Agricultural Statistics Service. As with many crop insurance policies for major crops, the expected price component of the guarantee for STAX is based on the average futures market price for cotton prior to planting time. In a previous farm bill proposal in 2012, specifically the 2012 House Agriculture Committee bill (H.R. 6083), a minimum price of $0.6861 per pound would have been used in the calculation of the insurance guarantee if it was higher than the expected market price. Inclusion of a minimum guarantee price would have provided enhanced the price protection for producers but would have introduced price supports into crop insurance and complicated the expected resolution of the cotton trade case.

[10] For numerical examples of SCO, see Nick Paulson, University of Illinois, Understanding the Supplemental Coverage Option (SCO) in the 2014 Farm Bill, March 12, 2014, http://www.farmdoc.illinois.edu/webinars/downloads/PDF/120314_farm_bill_sco_paulson.pdf.

[11] The two approaches differ in that ARC price guarantee is based on historical market prices while the crop insurance guarantees (including SCO) is based on expected market prices prior to planting. For more, see CRS Report R43448, Farm Commodity Provisions in the 2014 Farm Bill (P.L. 113-79).

[12] U.S. Department of Agriculture, FSA-RMA Farm Bill Listening Session, Washington, DC, March 27, 2014.

[13] AGR-Lite has maximum liability of $1 million compared with $6.5 million for AGR. AGR-Lite does not limit the share of livestock revenue in the guarantee (limited to 35% in AGR). Both products use a producer's five-year historical farm average revenue as reported on the Internal Revenue Service (IRS) tax return form (Schedule F or equivalent forms). Coverage levels range from 65% to 80% of historical revenue.

[14] USDA defines a limited resource farmer or rancher as one who has farm sales not more than $172,800 and household income at or below the national poverty level for a family of four. "Socially disadvantaged" means a group whose members have been subjected to racial or ethnic prejudice because of their identity as members of a group without regard to their individual qualities. (7 U.S.C. 2279(e)).

[15] In the House farm bill debate, prior to the floor vote on the farm bill on June 20, 2013 (which was rejected by a vote of 195-234), the House rejected H.Amdt. 216 by a vote of 208-217.

It would have limited premium subsidies to those producers with an adjusted gross income under $250,000, limited per-person premium subsidies to $50,000, and capped crop insurance providers' reimbursement of administrative and operating expenses at $900 million and reduced their rate of return to 12%.

In: Federal Crop Insurance
Editor: Tristan E. Bonner

ISBN: 978-1-63463-688-9

Chapter 3

CROP INSURANCE: CONSIDERATIONS IN REDUCING FEDERAL PREMIUM SUBSIDIES*

United States Government Accountability Office

ABBREVIATIONS

CBO	Congressional Budget Office
ERS	Economic Research Service
RMA	Risk Management Agency
USDA	U.S. Department of Agriculture

WHY GAO DID THIS STUDY

Federally subsidized crop insurance, which farmers can buy to help manage the risk inherent in farming, has become one of the most important programs in the farm safety net. Revenue policies, which protect farmers against crop revenue loss from declines in production or price, are the most

* This is an edited, reformatted and augmented version of The United States Government Accountability Office publication, GAO-14-700, dated August 2014.

popular policy type and account for nearly 80 percent of all premium subsidies. The crop insurance program's cost has come under scrutiny while the nation's budgetary pressures have been increasing.

GAO was asked to look at the cost of the crop insurance program. This report examines (1) trends in federal crop insurance costs and farm sector income and wealth from 2003 through 2012 and (2) the potential savings to the government and impacts on farmers, if any, of reducing federal premium subsidies for revenue policies. GAO analyzed USDA crop insurance program data and farm sector income and wealth data from 2003 through 2012 (most recent year with complete crop insurance data); reviewed economic literature and documents from stakeholders including farm industry groups and researchers; and interviewed USDA officials.

What GAO Recommends

To reduce the cost of the crop insurance program, Congress should consider reducing the level of federal premium subsidies for revenue crop insurance policies, including a phased reduction, if appropriate, and directing USDA to monitor and report on the impact, if any, of this reduction on crop insurance program participation. In written comments, USDA said it had no comments on the report's findings.

What GAO Found

The cost of the federal crop insurance program and farm sector income and wealth grew significantly from 2003 through 2012. The cost of crop insurance averaged $3.4 billion a year from fiscal years 2003 through 2007, but it increased to $8.4 billion a year for fiscal years 2008 through 2012. According to the U.S. Department of Agriculture's (USDA) Risk Management Agency (RMA), the agency that administers the crop insurance program, subsidies for crop insurance premiums accounted for $42.1 billion—or about 72 percent—of the $58.7 billion total program costs from 2003 through 2012. Revenue policies, the most frequently purchased crop insurance option, accounted for $30.9 billion of the total premium subsidy costs for 2003 through 2012. Crop insurance premium subsidy rates—the percentage of premiums paid by the government—are set by Congress and would require congressional action to be changed. For most policies, the rates range from 38 to 80 percent, depending on the policy type, coverage level chosen, and geographic diversity of crops insured. As premium subsidy costs increased, farm sector income and wealth indicators also increased. For example, for each year from 2003 through 2012, median farm household income exceeded median U.S. household income. Specifically, on average, median farm household income was $7,205, or 13.8 percent, greater each year than U.S. household income, in constant 2012 dollars. Farm sector income also grew from $73.8 billion in 2003 to $113.8 billion in 2012, in constant 2012 dollars. Farm real estate values, another measure of farm prosperity, increased by 72 percent from 2003 through 2012, in constant 2012 dollars, and farmers relied less on borrowed funds to finance their holdings.

Reducing premium subsidies for revenue policies could potentially result in hundreds of millions of dollars in annual budgetary savings with limited costs to individual farmers. For example, the federal government would have potentially saved more than $400 million in 2012 by reducing premium subsidies by 5 percentage points, and the savings would have been nearly $2 billion by reducing these subsidies by 20 percentage points. Although such reductions would have required farmers to pay more of their premiums, the impact on their average production costs per acre would have been limited, usually less than 2 percent, and often less than 1 percent. For example, for corn, premium subsidy reductions of 5 and 20 percentage points in 2012 would have raised average production costs per acre by about $2.80 and $11.20, respectively. These increases would have been about 0.4 percent and 1.7 percent, respectively, of the total average production cost per acre of $656 that year for corn. The ultimate impact of such limited production cost increases on farmers' income would depend on their individual profit margins. However, for the industry as a whole, the impact appears to be minimal. In 2000, when Congress enacted new premium subsidy rates, the new rates immediately became effective. In contrast, when RMA increases the premiums charged for policies, it generally phases in the increases over several years to lessen the impact on farmers. Documents from farm industry groups and some researchers note that reductions in premium subsidies could result in lower farmer participation in the program and lower insurance coverage levels. However, available economic literature indicates that farmers' response to such reductions may be small due to factors such as the attractiveness of revenue policies and increasing importance of crop insurance as other farm programs are reduced or eliminated. In addition, other stakeholders identified incentives that would help keep farmers in the program, including pressure from lenders to maintain crop insurance coverage and the importance of crop insurance to many farmers as their primary risk management tool. In the event that subsidy rates were reduced, actual information on the impact on farmer participation would be available if participation were monitored.

* * *

August 8, 2014

The Honorable Tom Coburn, M.D.
Ranking Member
Committee on Homeland Security and Governmental Affairs
United States Senate

Dear Dr. Coburn:

Federally subsidized crop insurance, which farmers can purchase to help manage the risk inherent in farming, has become one of the most important programs in the farm safety net, according to USDA officials and some farm industry stakeholders. Under the federal crop insurance program, farmers can choose various levels and types of insurance protection. For example, they can insure against losses caused by poor crop yields or declines in revenues for each insurable crop they produce. In 2012, the crop insurance program provided more than $117 billion in insurance coverage for about 283 million acres of farmland with almost 1.2 million policies. The federal government's crop insurance costs include subsidies to pay for (1) part of a farmer's crop insurance premiums, which averaged about 62 percent of total premiums in 2012, and (2) administrative and operating expenses (administrative costs)—provided on behalf of farmers—to insurance companies to cover their expenses for selling and servicing crop insurance policies.

In recent years, policies that protect against crop revenue loss resulting from declines in production, price, or both—known as revenue policies— have become the most popular policy type. For example, as of 2012, the majority of crop insurance policies—almost 70 percent—was revenue policies, and they accounted for nearly 80 percent of all premium subsidies. In general, these policies include a harvest price provision, allowing farmers with this coverage whose insured crops experience a decline in revenue below the level guaranteed in their policy to file a loss claim based on the higher of either the preplanting price or the harvest price of the covered crop.

The cost of the federal crop insurance program has come under scrutiny at the same time that the nation's budgetary pressures have been increasing. As of March 2014, the national debt was estimated at $17.6 trillion.[1] Furthermore, in the last 15 years, debt held by the public has nearly doubled. As we discuss on our key issues website,[2] the large national debt reduces the federal government's flexibility to respond to new and unexpected challenges and, if interest rates rise, the payments on the debt will use up a growing part of the federal budget. Furthermore, increased attention to future fiscal exposures—responsibilities, programs, and activities that legally commit or create the expectation of future funding—that could affect the federal government's fiscal condition is made more important because of the nation's longer term fiscal challenges. In the past, we have identified numerous opportunities for the federal government to save tax dollars and enhance revenue, including in the federal crop insurance program.[3]

In this context, you asked us to look at the cost of the federal crop insurance program, specifically concerning the costs associated with revenue insurance policies. This report examines (1) trends in federal crop insurance costs and farm sector income and wealth from 2003 through 2012 and (2) the potential savings to the government and impacts on farmers, if any, of reducing federal premium subsidies for revenue policies.

To address these objectives, we interviewed officials of the U.S. Department of Agriculture (USDA), including officials from the Economic Research Service (ERS) and Risk Management Agency (RMA), and reviewed documents they provided, including, for example, documents on crop insurance program costs and outlays. We also interviewed officials at the Congressional Budget Office (CBO). For the first objective, we reviewed and analyzed RMA crop insurance program data for 2003 through 2012,[4] including data on the types of crops insured, the number of acres insured, and total program costs. In particular, we focused on these data as they relate to revenue policies. For these analyses we only included information on "buy-up" policies—that is, the portion of crop insurance for which a farmer pays a premium; "buy-up" policies account for any coverage that is purchased above the "catastrophic" level.[5] We also reviewed and analyzed ERS data for 2003 through 2012 on the overall financial condition of the farm sector, including data on farm income and farmland values. For the purposes of this report, crop insurance costs and premium subsidies, which are budget-related data, are reported in nominal dollars, while data on median farm household and U.S. household income, net farm and net cash income, and farmland values are reported in inflation adjusted dollars, using 2012 as the reference year. In addition, as appropriate, we report these data in calendar, fiscal, or crop years,[6] depending on how the data were reported in the source documents. Unless otherwise indicated, these data are in calendar years. To address the second objective, we analyzed the potential impacts of reducing premium subsides for revenue policies in 2012, the most recent year for which we had complete data at the time of our analysis. Using RMA data, we estimated what the savings to the federal government would have been if premium subsidies had been reduced by 5, 10, 15, or 20 percentage points in 2012. We also estimated what a reduction in premium subsidies by each amount would have added to the production costs of farmers. Specifically, using ERS Agricultural Resource Management Survey data, we estimated what the additional production cost per acre, on average, would have been in 2012 for a variety of crops, including the major field crops of corn, cotton, soybeans, and wheat that receive the majority of the revenue crop insurance premium subsidies. We reviewed related documentation, interviewed knowledgeable agency officials, and reviewed related internal controls information to evaluate the reliability of the data discussed above. In each case, we concluded that the data were sufficiently reliable for the purposes of this report. In addition, we reviewed the agricultural economic literature for the period 1993 through 2013,[7] to get information on what impact, if any, premium subsidy reductions would have on farmers' participation in the crop insurance program. A more detailed discussion of our objectives, scope, and methodology is presented in appendix I.

We conducted this performance audit from May 2013 to August 2014 in accordance with generally accepted government auditing standards. Those standards require that we plan and perform the audit to obtain sufficient, appropriate evidence to provide a reasonable basis for our findings and conclusions based on our audit objectives. We believe that the evidence obtained provides a reasonable basis for our findings and conclusions based on our objectives.

BACKGROUND

Farmers are exposed to financial losses because of production risks—droughts, floods, and other natural disasters—as well as variations in the market price of their crops. The federal government has played an active role in helping to mitigate the effects of these risks on farm income by promoting the use of crop insurance. RMA has overall responsibility for administering the federal crop insurance program, including controlling costs and protecting against fraud, waste, and abuse. As of May 2014, RMA partnered with 19 private insurance companies that sell and service the program's insurance policies and share a percentage of the risk of loss and opportunity for gain associated with the policies (known as "underwriting"). RMA administers the crop insurance program through a Standard Reinsurance Agreement that establishes the terms and conditions under which participating insurance companies sell and service federal crop insurance policies.

Through the federal crop insurance program, farmers insure against losses on more than 100 crops. These crops include major crops—such as corn, cotton, soybeans, and wheat, which accounted for more than three-quarters of the acres enrolled in the program in 2012—as well as nursery crops and certain fruits and vegetables. More specifically, according to RMA, federal crop insurance penetration based on planted acres is high for the principal crops of corn, soybeans, wheat, and cotton.[8] For example, in 2012, about 84 percent of the planted principal crops were insured under the federal crop insurance program. More specifically, corn acreage was 84 percent insured, soybean acreage was 84 percent insured, wheat acreage was 83 percent insured, and cotton acreage was 94 percent insured.

Most crop insurance policies are either production-based or revenue policies. For production-based policies, a farmer can receive a payment if there is a production loss relative to the farmer's historical production per acre. Revenue policies protect against crop revenue loss resulting from declines in production, price, or both. The federal government encourages farmers' participation in the federal crop insurance program by subsidizing the insurance premiums and acting as the primary reinsurer for the private insurance companies that take on the risk of covering, or underwriting, losses of participating farmers.

The federal government's premium subsidies for crop insurance policies are not payments to farmers, but they can be considered a financial benefit to farmers. Without a premium subsidy, a participating farmer would have to pay the full amount of the policy premium. Congress sets premium subsidy rates, meaning the percentage of the premium paid by the government. Premium subsidy rates vary by the level of insurance coverage that the farmer chooses and the geographic diversity of crops insured. For most policies, the statutory premium subsidy rates range from 38 percent to 80 percent. Premium subsidy rates increased, as a percentage of total premiums, from an average of 37 percent in 2000 to an average of 63 percent in 2012. In addition, premium subsidies rose as crop prices increased because higher prices meant the insured value of the crop increased, and premiums are based on the value of what is insured.

In addition, the federal government pays administrative and operating expense subsidies to insurance companies as an allowance that is intended to cover their expenses for selling and servicing crop insurance policies. In turn, insurance companies use these subsidies to cover their overhead expenses, such as payroll and rent, and to pay commissions to insurance agencies and their agents. Insurance companies also incur expenses associated with verifying—also called adjusting—the amount of loss claimed. These expenses include, for example, loss adjusters' compensation and travel expenses of adjusters to farmers' fields. The administrative expense subsidies also can be considered a subsidy to farmers; with these subsidies, crop insurance premiums are lower than they would otherwise be if the program followed commercial insurance practices. In private insurance, such as automobile insurance, these administrative expenses typically are captured through the premiums paid by all policyholders.

The federal government provides crop insurance premium subsidies in part to achieve high crop insurance participation and coverage levels.[9] Higher participation and coverage levels may reduce or eliminate the need for disaster assistance payments from congressionally authorized ad hoc disaster programs to help farmers recover from natural disasters, which can be costly. For example, under three separate congressionally authorized ad hoc disaster programs, USDA provided $7 billion in payments to farmers whose crops were damaged or destroyed by natural disasters from 2001 to 2007. Farmers' participation in the federal crop insurance program and spending on ad hoc disaster assistance have been policy issues for more than 30 years. A 2005 USDA publication[10] asserts that Congress passed the Federal Crop Insurance Act of 1980 and subsequent related legislation to strengthen participation in the crop insurance program with the goal of replacing costly disaster assistance programs. According to this publication, the government has historically attempted to increase participation in the federal crop insurance program by subsidizing premiums, including increasing the level of these subsidies over time.

The 2014 farm bill introduced several changes to the crop insurance program. Regarding revenue policies specifically, the legislation added peanuts to the list of crops eligible for this policy type. The legislation also made "enterprise units" a permanent option for revenue and other policy types. An enterprise unit consists of all insurable acreage of the same insured crop in the county in which the farmer has a share on the date coverage begins for the crop year. In addition, separate insurable enterprise units for both irrigated and nonirrigated crops will be available. Separating the acreage can increase risk protection for farmers because losses on dryland crops would no longer be offset by higher yields on irrigated acreage when the two are combined.

The 2014 farm bill also added two new policy options to the crop insurance program—the Supplemental Coverage Option and the Stacked Income Protection Plan for upland cotton. The Supplemental Coverage Option is based on expected county yields or revenue, to cover part of the deductible under the farmer's underlying policy (referred to as a farmer's out-of-pocket loss or "shallow loss"). The federal subsidy as a share of the policy premium is set at 65 percent. The Stacked Income Protection Plan insures against losses in county revenue of 10 to 30 percent of expected county revenue based on the deductible level selected by the farmer for the underlying individual policy. The federal subsidy as a share of the policy premium is set at 80 percent. As of June 2014, USDA was developing implementing guidance for these new policies that it expects to issue before the start of the 2015 crop year. For now, it is uncertain how farmers will utilize these new policies and how their use will impact federal crop insurance premium costs, including for revenue policy premium subsides.

Federal Crop Insurance Costs and Farm Sector Income and Wealth Grew Significantly from 2003 through 2012

Federal crop insurance program costs and farm sector income and wealth grew significantly during the period 2003 through 2012. Costs of federal crop insurance are growing due to an increase in premium subsidies, particularly for revenue policies. Farmers are increasingly purchasing revenue policies and are choosing higher coverage levels for these policies. Meanwhile, indicators of farm business economic well-being— such as farm income and real estate and asset values—all increased from 2003 through 2012.

Costs of Federal Corp Insurance Are Growing, Primarily Due to an Increase in Premium Subsidies for Revenue Policies

The cost of the federal crop insurance program grew significantly from 2003 through 2012, according to our analysis of RMA data. For fiscal years 2003 through 2007, federal crop insurance costs averaged $3.4 billion a year, but for fiscal years 2008 through 2012, the crop insurance program cost an average of $8.4 billion a year. There were significant drought and crop losses in crop year 2012 that contributed to the spike in government costs to $14.1 billion. These trends are shown in figure 1. According to an April 2014 CBO estimate, for fiscal years 2014 through 2023, program costs are expected to average $8.9 billion annually.

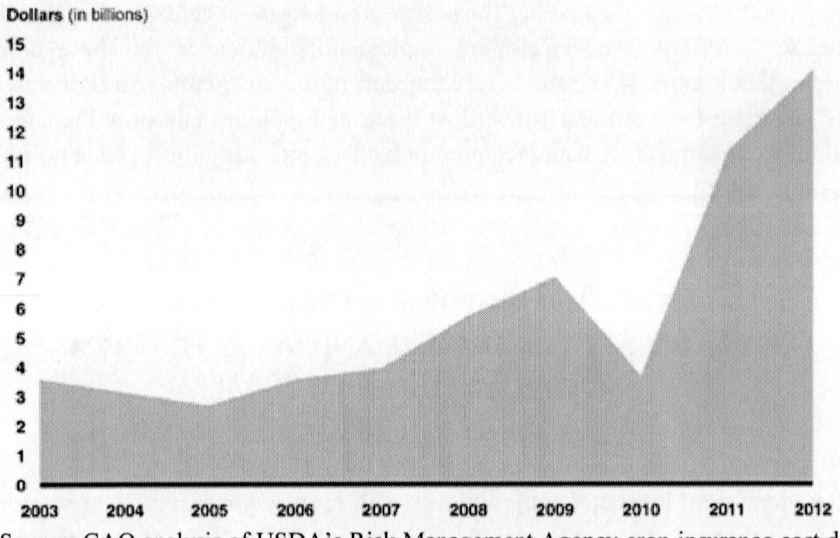

Source: GAO analysis of USDA's Risk Management Agency crop insurance cost data and Federal Crop Insurance Corporation audited financial statements. GAO-147-700.

Note: In general, the decline in costs in 2010 was related to strong yields due to favorable weather conditions and lower crop prices, and the increase in 2011 and 2012 reflects crop losses due to drought and higher crop prices.

Figure 1. Federal Crop Insurance Costs, Fiscal Years 2003 through 2012.

In fiscal years 2003 through 2012, according to our analysis of RMA data, premium subsidies comprised approximately $42.1 billion of $58.7 billion in total government costs for federal crop insurance, or almost 72 percent of total program costs. Revenue policy premium subsidies specifically accounted for $30.9 billion of the premium subsidy costs over that period. RMA offered 17 different crop insurance policies in crop year 2012, but revenue policies were the most frequently purchased and accounted for the majority of all premium subsidies. For example, for crop year 2012, revenue policy premium subsidies cost $5.5 billion that year, which accounted for 82 percent of the $6.7 billion in total premium subsidy costs to the government. Figure 2 shows the breakdown of costs for the overall crop insurance program into premium subsidies; administrative and operating expense subsidies; and other costs, such as the salaries of RMA staff, research and development initiatives for new crop insurance products, and the net underwriting loss for the period, for fiscal years 2003 through 2012.

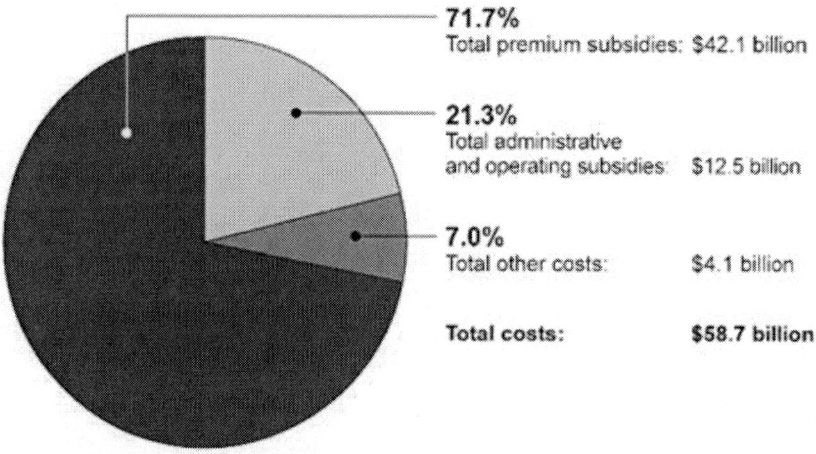

Source: GAO analysis of USDA's Risk Management Agency crop insurance cost data and Federal Crop Insurance Corporation audited financial statements. GAO-147-700.

Figure 2. Breakdown of Federal Crop Insurance Costs, Overall, for Fiscal Years 2003 through 2012.

Farmers Are Increasingly Purchasing Revenue Policies and Choosing Higher Insurance Coverage Levels

As shown in figure 3, overall crop insurance premium subsidies more than tripled from $1.8 billion to $6.7 billion from crop years 2003 through 2012.

The revenue policy premium subsidies increased from $1.1 billion in crop year 2003 to $5.5 billion in crop year 2012, a nearly 5-fold increase.

The total acreage covered by federal crop insurance also continued to increase from crop year 2003 through crop year 2012, from around 183.7 million acres in 2003 to 265.2 million acres in 2012. As shown in figure 4, the amount of that acreage covered by revenue policies also increased, from about 112.2 million acres in 2003 to 180.9 million acres in 2012. In 2012, revenue policies were purchased for about 68 percent of the acres covered by federal crop insurance.

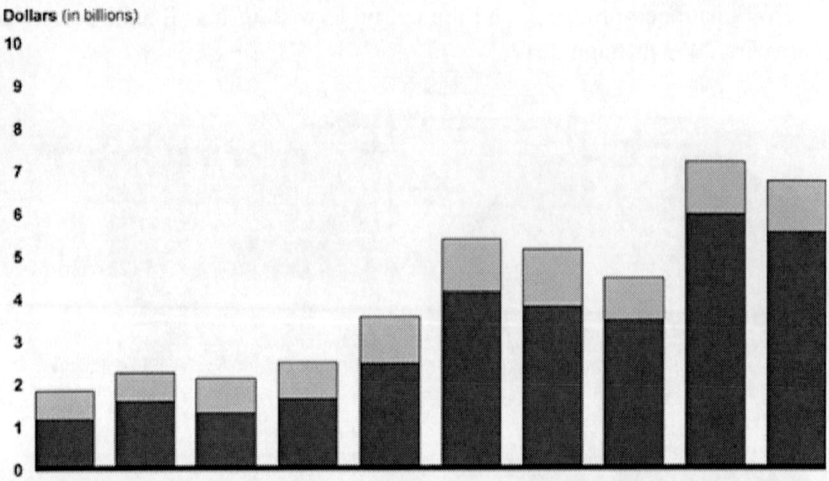

Source: GAO analysis of USDA's Risk Management Agency crop insurance data. GAO-14-700.

Figure 3. Federal Premium Subsidies for Revenue and Other Crop Insurance Policies, Crop Years 2003 through 2012.

The total acreage covered by federal crop insurance also continued to increase from crop year 2003 through crop year 2012, from around 183.7 million acres in 2003 to 265.2 million acres in 2012. As shown in figure 4, the amount of that acreage covered by revenue policies also increased, from about 112.2 million acres in 2003 to 180.9 million acres in 2012. In 2012, revenue policies were purchased for about 68 percent of the acres covered by federal crop insurance.

Farmers have also increased their purchases of higher coverage levels of crop insurance—that is, the percentage of their normal annual revenue that they want to insure—for their revenue policies.

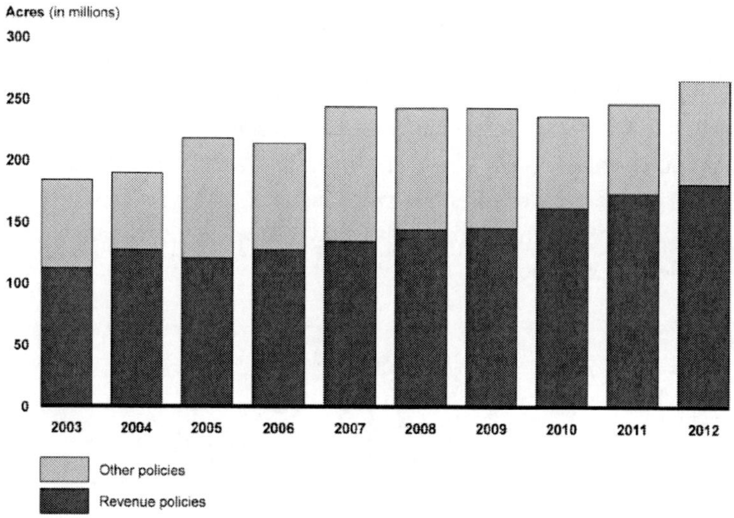

Source: GAO analysis of USDA's Risk Management Agency crop insurance data. GAO-14-700.

Figure 4. Acres Covered with Revenue and Other Crop Insurance Policies, Crop Years 2003 through 2012.

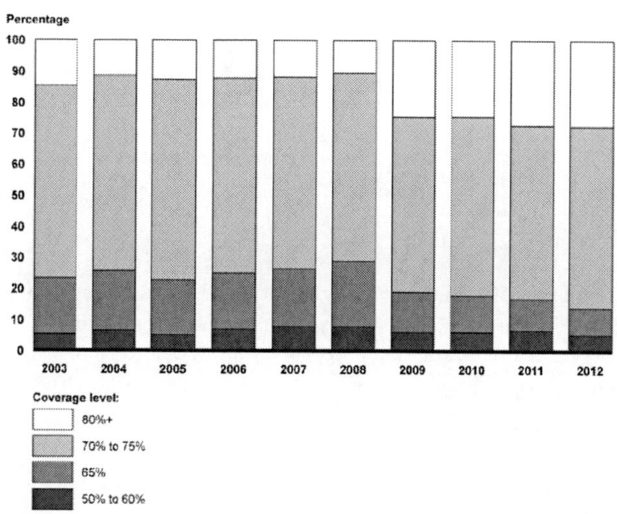

Source: GAO analysis of USDA's Risk Management Agency crop insurance data. GAO-14-700.

Figure 5. Percentage of Acres Insured with Revenue Crop Insurance Policies by Coverage Level, Crop Years 2003 through 2012.

These higher coverage levels equate to greater potential liability for the government and insurers in the case of loss and higher premium levels for the policies, both of which contribute to higher program costs. According to our analysis of RMA data, the percentage of acres insured at higher coverage levels has increased in recent years, as shown in figure 5. For example, in crop year 2003, 14.7 percent of all acres were insured under revenue policies at a coverage level of 80 percent or greater. By crop year 2012, that figure had nearly doubled, to 27.6 percent.[11]

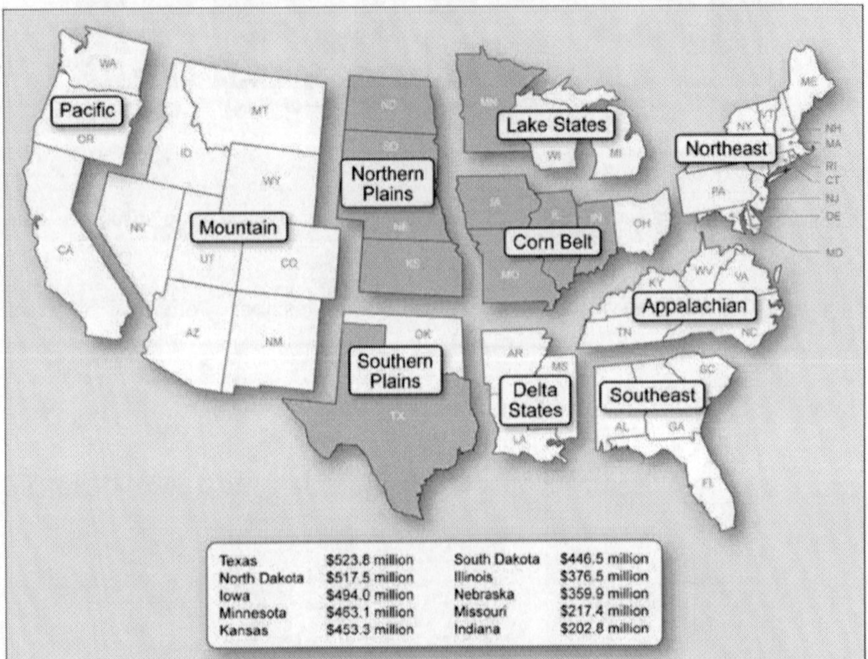

Source: GAO analysis of USDA's Risk Management Agency crop insurance data and National Agricultural Statistics Service economic region data; map resources (map). GAO-14-700.

Note: The map also shows how the 48 continental states fall into 10 major economic regions determined by USDA.

Figure 6. Top 10 States Receiving Revenue Crop Insurance Premium Subsidies in Crop Year 2012.

Our analysis of RMA data showed that farmers in 10 states accounted for the majority of revenue policies purchased and, as a result, a majority of the premium subsidies in crop year 2012. As shown in figure 6, these 10 states in descending order of subsidy amounts received were Texas, North Dakota, Iowa, Minnesota, Kansas, South Dakota, Illinois, Nebraska, Missouri, and Indiana. Combined, they received almost $4.1 billion in revenue premium subsidies in crop year 2012, which was approximately 73.5 percent of the total amount of federal premium subsidies for revenue policies for that year. In crop year 2012, Texas led all states in premium subsidies, with farmers receiving more than $523.8 million in revenue premium subsidies for the approximately 11 million acres covered by revenue policies; over 60 percent of these premium subsidies and almost half of the acres covered were for cotton.

The list of crops eligible for revenue policy insurance coverage has continued to grow.[12] Table 1 shows which crops were eligible to receive revenue policy premium subsidies from crop year 2003 through crop year 2012. In crop year 2013, dry beans and dry peas also became eligible for revenue policy insurance.[13] According to RMA documents, the estimated cost of these two additional crops was $28.3 million in revenue premium subsidies for crop year 2013. Further, as discussed, peanuts will be eligible for revenue policy coverage starting in crop year 2015.

Table 1. Crops Eligible to Receive Revenue Crop Insurance Premium Subsidies, Crop Years 2003 through 2012

Dollars (in millions)

Crop	Total revenue premium subsidies, 2003 through 2012
Corn	$13,671.6
Soybeans	$7,702.9
Wheat	$5,860.9
Cotton	$2,373.2
Grain sorghum	$632.7
Sunflowers	$248.3
Canola	$173.8
Rice	$124.9
Barley	$117.2
Popcorn	$2.5

Source: GAO analysis of USDA's Risk Management Agency crop insurance data. | GAO-14-700.

Farm Income, Real Estate, and Asset Values Increased from 2003 through 2012

The farm economy improved from 2003 through 2012, and 2012 was a record year for farm income, due in part to high crop prices. For example, median farm household income rose from 2003 to 2012 and was higher than the median income for all U.S. households every year during this period, according to ERS data.[14] More specifically, on average, median farm household income was $7,205, or 13.8 percent, more than median U.S. household income annually during this time period (in constant 2012 dollars that reflect adjustments for inflation). Median farm household income was 33.9 percent higher than median income for all U.S. households in 2012—$68,298 compared with $51,017. Households associated with farms specializing in cash grains such as corn or soybeans had a median household income of about $82,300 in 2012, and median household income was even higher for those farms specializing in rice, tobacco, cotton, or peanuts, at about $101,400 in 2012. Figure 7 shows the median income for farm households and for U.S. households from 2003 through 2012, in constant 2012 dollars that reflect adjustments for inflation.

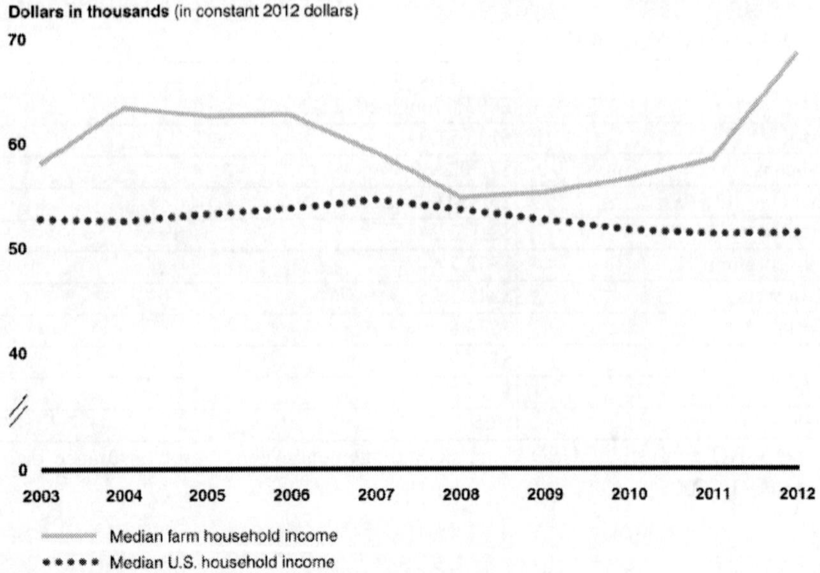

Source: USDA's Economic Research Service. GAO-14-700.

Figure 7. Median Farm and U.S. Household Income, 2003 through 2012.

Farm sector income also grew from $73.8 billion in 2003 to $113.8 billion in 2012. Net farm and net cash income for U.S. farms from 2003 through 2012 (in constant 2012 dollars that reflect adjustments for inflation) are shown in figure 8. Net farm income is the value of the agricultural goods produced by farm operators less the costs of inputs and services. Net cash income is the cash earned from the sale of these agricultural goods and the conversion of farm assets into cash.

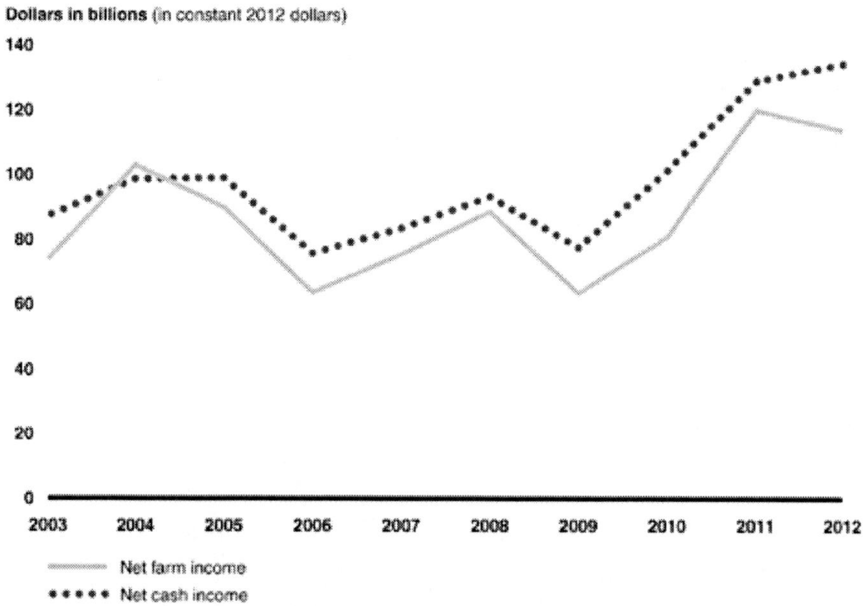

Source: USDA's Economic Research Service. GAO-14-700.

Note: Net farm income is the value of the agricultural goods produced by farm operators less the costs of inputs and *services. Net* cash income is the cash earned from the sale of these agricultural goods and the conversion of farm assets into cash.

Figure 8. Net Farm and Cash Income for U.S. Farms, 2003 through 2012.

According to ERS data, however, net farm and net cash income are forecast to decrease in 2014, due principally to falling crop prices as compared with prior years. Net farm income is forecast to go up to $130.5 billion in 2013, and then decline to $95.8 billion, or by about 26.6 percent in 2014. The 2014 forecast would be the lowest since 2010, but it would still be $8 billion above the average of years 2004 to 2013. After adjusting for inflation, 2013's net farm income would be the highest since 1973, and the 2014 net farm income forecast would be the seventh highest. Net cash income is forecast at $101.9 billion for 2014, down almost 22 percent from the 2013 forecast of $130.1.[15]

Farm real estate—a measurement of the value of all land and buildings on farms—accounted for 82 percent of the total value of U.S. farm assets in 2012. Because farm real estate comprises such a significant portion of the farm's balance sheet, a change in the value of farm real estate is a strong indicator of the farm sector's financial performance. U.S. farm real estate values increased by 72 percent from 2003 through 2012 due to high farm income and low interest rates, according to USDA data. Farm real estate value averaged $2,650 per acre for 2012, and the highest farm real estate values were in the Corn Belt region at $5,560 per acre.[16] According to USDA data, this increase in national farm real estate values is forecast to continue, with an estimated average value of $2,900 per acre in 2013, up 9.4 percent from 2012 values. National farm real estate values for 2003 through 2012 (in constant 2012 dollars that reflect adjustments for inflation) are shown in figure 9.

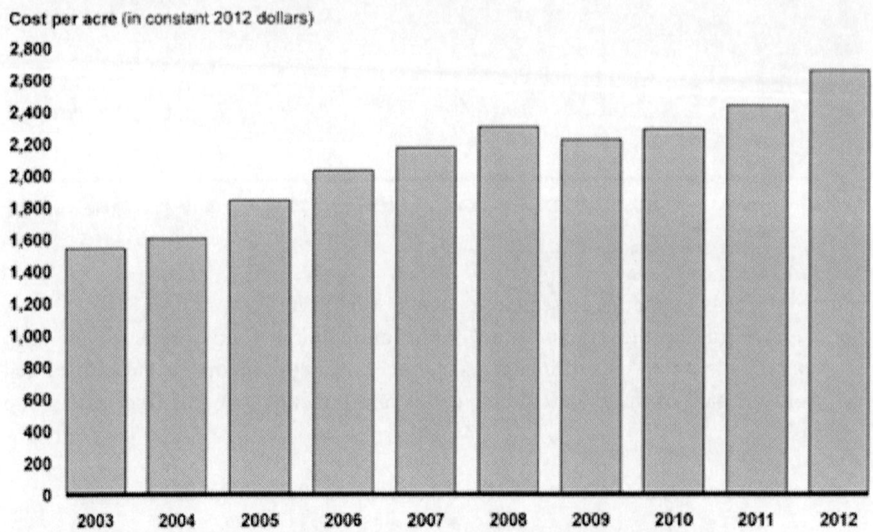

Source: USDA'a National Agriculture Statistics Service. GAO-14-700.

Figure 9. National Farm Real Estate Values, Average per Acre, 2003 through 2012.

According to ERS documents, a farm's debt-to-equity ratio and the debt-to-asset ratio are also major indicators of the financial well-being of the farm sector. The debt-to-equity ratio measures the relative proportion of funds invested by creditors (debt) and owners (equity). The debt-to-asset ratio measures the proportion of farm business assets that are financed through debt. Lower ratios signify that farmers are relying less on borrowed funds to finance their asset holdings. Farmers' debt-to-equity ratio fell from 15.7 percent in 2003 to 12.0 percent in 2012, and their debtto-asset ratio fell from 13.6 percent in 2003 to 10.7 percent in 2012. The farm sector's debt-to-equity and debt-to-asset ratios are forecast to continue a pattern of decline, falling to an estimated 11.8 and 10.5 percent in 2014, respectively. According to ERS documents, these decreases would result in the lowest ratios for both measurements since 1954. The historically low levels of farm debt, relative to equity and assets, attest to the sector's strong financial position. ERS documents state that this also means the sector is better insulated from risks such as adverse weather, changing macroeconomic conditions in the United States and abroad, or fluctuations in farm asset values that may occur due to changing demand for agricultural assets. The steady decline in both ratios since the mid-1980s is due to relatively large growth in the value of farm assets, driven principally, according to ERS documents, by the increases in farm real estate values. Figure 10 shows these farm sector debt ratios from 2003 through 2012.

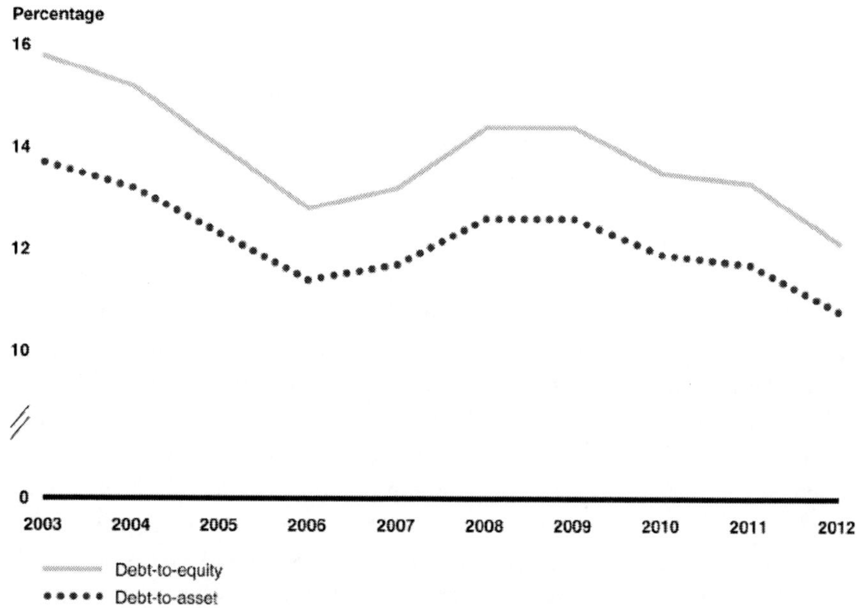

Source: USDA's Economic Research Service. GAO-14-700.

Figure 10. Farm Sector Debt Ratios, 2003 through 2012.

Reducing Federal Premium Subsidies for Revenue Policies Would Potentially Save Millions of Dollars with Limited Costs to Individual Farmers

According to our analysis of RMA data, the federal government would have potentially saved more than $400 million in 2012 by reducing premium subsidies on federal crop insurance revenue policies by 5 percentage points, and the savings would have been nearly $2 billion with a 20 percentage point premium subsidy reduction. Premium subsidy reductions of 5 to 20 percentage points would have in turn raised farmers' average production costs per acre from about $1.90 to about $16.90 for crops such as corn, soybeans, and cotton.[17] As a percentage of the total production cost per acre, these increases would usually have been less than 2 percent and often less than 1 percent. Because farmers would be required to pay more for their crop insurance, reduced federal premium subsidies for revenue policies could affect the participation rate in the crop insurance program. However, the magnitude of the impact on farmers' participation as a result of lower federal premium subsidies for revenue policies may be minimal.

A 5 Percentage Point Reduction in Federal Premium Subsidies for Revenue Policies Would Potentially Save Millions, and Larger Reductions Would Save More

Reducing premium subsidies for revenue policies would potentially result in significant savings to the federal government, according to our analysis of RMA data. For example, if the premium subsidies paid in 2012 had been reduced by 5, 10, 15, or 20 percentage points that year, the potential savings for corn would have been about $197 million, $394 million, $592 million, or $789 million, respectively. Moreover, for the 10 crops—barley, canola, corn, cotton, grain sorghum, popcorn, rice, soybeans, sunflowers, and wheat—that accounted for virtually 100 percent of the premium subsidies paid for revenue policies in 2012, the potential savings with those levels of premium subsidy reductions would have been about $439 million, $878 million, $1.3 billion, and $1.8 billion, respectively. In 2000, when Congress enacted legislation to increase crop insurance premium subsidy rates, the new rates immediately became effective (i.e., upon enactment of the legislation).[18] In contrast, according to RMA officials, when the agency increases the premiums charged for crop insurance policies based on new actuarial data, as it did in 2012, it generally phases in the increases over several years so the impact on farmers is less dramatic.[19] Table 2 provides more information on the amount of potential savings that corresponds to the various levels of reduction in revenue policy premium subsidies, by crop.

Table 2. Potential Savings from Reducing Federal Premium Subsidies for Revenue Policies, by Crop, for 2012 Dollars

Dollars (in millions)

Crop	Percentage of total revenue policy premium subsidies received in 2012	Savings from 5 point subsidy reduction	Savings from 10 point subsidy reduction	Savings from 15 point subsidy reduction	Savings from20 point subsidyreduction
Barley	0.6%	$2.5	$5.0	$7.5	$10.0
Canola	0.7%	$3.2	$6.3	$9.5	$12.6
Corn	44.7%	$197.2	$394.4	$591.6	$788.8
Cotton	8.6%	$36.0	$72.0	$108.0	$143.9
Grain sorghum	1.9%	$8.3	$16.5	$24.8	$33.0
Popcorn	0.0%	$0.2	$0.5	$0.7	$1.0
Rice	0.4%	$1.4	$2.8	$4.2	$5.6
Soybeans	24.3%	$106.6	$213.3	$319.9	$426.5
Sunflowers	0.8%	$3.4	$6.7	$10.1	$13.5
Wheat	18.0%	$80.2	$160.5	$240.7	$320.9
Total	100.0%	$438.9	$877.9	$1,316.8	$1,755.8

Source: GAO analysis of USDA's Risk Management Agency crop insurance data. | GAO-14-700

Note: The higher savings amounts for some crops correspond to the greater share of total revenue policy premium subsidies received by these crops. These savings amounts also represent the increase in total farm costs as a result of the subsidy rate reductions.

These levels of potential savings are based on the assumption that farmers would not make any changes to their policies. For example, according to this assumption, farmers would not change from a revenue policy to a less expensive yield policy or leave the crop insurance program altogether. In addition, they are based on the assumption that farmers would keep their existing coverage levels. To the extent that farmers purchased less expensive policies, left the program, or purchased lower coverage levels, the potential savings would be greater because the total amount of federal premium subsidies required would decrease. In addition, the potential savings would decline if crop prices declined. This would occur because premiums are affected by crop prices—as crop prices decrease so does the value of the crops being insured, which results in lower crop insurance premiums. Since premium subsidies are a set percentage of the premiums, these subsidy amounts would decrease as premium amounts decreased.

We and other federal agencies have previously analyzed the potential savings to the federal government from reductions in premium subsidies to all or selected crop insurance policies. In our March 2012 report, based on an analysis of RMA data, we found that if the premium subsidy rates of all participating farmers in 2010 and 2011 had been reduced by 10 percentage points—from 62 percent to 52 percent—the annual cost savings for those years would have been about $759 million and $1.2 billion, respectively.[20]

The president's 2013 budget, which included a proposal to reduce premium subsidies, asserts that deep premium subsidies are no longer needed with the current high farmer participation rates in the crop insurance program. Further, in his 2014 budget, the president included two legislative proposals to reduce the premium subsidies to farmers. One proposal was to reduce the premium subsidies by 3 percentage points for all yield and revenue policies that had premium subsidy rates above 50 percent. According to the RMA's analysis for this proposal, the premium subsidy reduction would save the federal government about $4.2 billion over 10 years. The second proposal was to reduce premium subsidies for revenue policies by 2 percentage points.[21] RMA estimated that this reduction in premium subsidies would save the government about $3.2 billion over a 10-year time frame. The president made a similar proposal in his 2015 budget but increased the subsidy rate reduction for revenue policies to 4 percent. RMA estimated the total expected savings over 10 years from that proposal would be $6.3 billion. However, any change in the premium subsidies would require action by Congress.

In a 2013 report containing options for reducing the deficit, CBO also discussed a reduction in the federal government's premium subsidy for crop insurance policies.[22] According to the CBO report, of the total crop insurance premiums, the federal government pays about 60 percent, on average, and the farmers pay about 40 percent. CBO's option proposed that those payment shares be reversed, with the government paying 40 percent, and the farmers being responsible for 60 percent. If this option were implemented, CBO estimated the federal government would save $22.1 billion over a 10-year period from 2014 through 2023.

Reducing Federal Premium Subsidies Would Increase Individual Farmers' Average Costs per Acre, but the Increase Would Be Limited

Reductions to revenue policy premium subsidies of 5, 10, 15, and 20 percentage points would result in increases in farmers' production costs as the share of the premium that they pay would increase. However, our analysis of 2012 RMA crop insurance data indicates that changes in average production costs would be limited. For example, individual corn farmers would have experienced average premium cost increases per acre for their crop insurance policies of $2.81, $5.62, $8.43, or $11.24 with premium subsidy reductions of 5, 10, 15, or 20 percentage points, respectively, in 2012. Those premium cost increases represent a limited increase in the average production costs per acre for corn farmers, usually less than 2 percent and often less than 1 percent. For example, the average production costs for corn farmers were about $656 per acre that year; with the premium cost increases, their production costs would have increased an average of 0.4 percent, 0.9 percent, 1.3 percent, and 1.7 percent with premium subsidy reductions of 5, 10, 15, or 20 percentage points, respectively. Table 3 provides information on the additional average per-acre premium costs per farmer and as a percentage of the average per-acre costs of production with premium subsidy reductions of 5 and 10 percentage points, and table 4 reflects those calculations with premium subsidy reductions of 15 and 20 percentage points. Both tables are for 2012.

Table 3. Estimated Increases in Farmer Production Costs Resulting from Federal Premium Subsidy Reductions of 5 and 10 Percentage Points, on Average per Acre and by Crop, 2012

Crop	Percentage of total revenue policy premium subsidies received in 2012	Average cost of production per acre	Average farmer premium increase per acre with 5 point subsidy reduction	Average increase in farmer premium as a percentage of cost of production for 5 point reduction	Average farmer premium increase per acre with 10 point subsidy reduction	Averageincrease infarmer premiumas a percentageof cost ofproduction for10 pointreduction
Barley	0.6%	$421.44	$1.92	0.5%	$3.84	0.9%
Canola	0.7%	a	$2.07	b	$4.15	b
Corn	44.7%	$655.79	$2.81	0.4%	$5.62	0.9%
Cotton	8.6%	$808.38	$4.23	0.5%	$8.47	1.0%

Table 3. (Continued)

Crop	Percentage of total revenue policy premium subsidies received in 2012	Average cost of production per acre	Average farmer premium increase per acre with 5 point subsidy reduction	Average increase in farmer premium as a percentage of cost of production for 5 point reduction	Average farmer premium increase per acre with 10 point subsidy reduction	Averageincrease infarmer premiumas a percentageof cost ofproduction for10 pointreduction
Grain sorghum	1.9%	$308.57	$2.51	0.8%	$5.02	1.6%
Popcorn	0.0%	a	$3.23	b	$6.45	b
Rice	0.4%	$985.85	$2.16	0.2%	$4.33	0.4%
Soybeans	24.3%	$417.38	$1.92	0.5%	$3.84	0.9%
Sun-flowers	0.8%	a	$2.33	b	$4.65	b
Wheat	18.0%	$303.78	$2.09	0.7%	$4.18	1.4%

Sources: GAO analysis of USDA's Risk Management Agency crop insurance data and Economic Research Service (ERS) cost of production data. | GAO-14-700.

[a] These data are not available because, according to ERS officials, USDA is not required to collect such data for these crops.

[b] We could not calculate the cost increases as a percentage of the production costs for these crops because of the missing data.

Table 4. Estimated Increases in Farmer Production Costs Resulting from Federal Premium Subsidy Reductions of 15 and 20 Percentage Points, on Average per Acre and by Crop, 2012

Crop	Percentage of total revenue policy subsidies received in 2012	Average cost of production per acre	Average farmer premium increase per acre with 15 point subsidy reduction	Average increase in farmer premium as a percentage of cost of production for 15 point reduction	Average farmer premium increase per acre with 20 point subsidy reduction	Average increasein farmerpremium as apercentage ofcost ofproduction for 20point reduction
Barley	0.6%	$421.44	$5.76	1.4%	$7.69	1.8%
Canola	0.7%	a	$6.22	b	$8.29	b
Corn	44.7%	$655.79	$8.43	1.3%	$11.24	1.7%
Cotton	8.6%	$808.38	$12.70	1.6%	$16.94	2.1%
Grain sorghum	1.9%	$308.57	$7.53	2.4%	$10.03	3.3%
Popcorn	0.0%	a	$9.68	b	$12.91	b

Crop	Percentage of total revenue policy subsidies received in 2012	Average cost of production per acre	Average farmer premium increase per acre with 15 point subsidy reduction	Average increase in farmer premium as a percentage of cost of production for 15 point reduction	Average farmer premium increase per acre with 20 point subsidy reduction	Average increasein farmerpremium as apercentage ofcost ofproduction for 20point reduction
Rice	0.4%	$985.85	$6.49	0.7%	$8.66	0.9%
Soybeans	24.3%	$417.38	$5.76	1.4%	$7.68	1.8%
Sunflowers	0.8%	a	$6.98	b	$9.31	b
Wheat	18.0%	$303.78	$6.26	2.1%	$8.35	2.7%

Sources: GAO analysis of USDA's Risk Management Agency crop insurance data and Economic Research Service (ERS) cost of production data. | GAO-14-700

[a] These data are not available because, according to ERS officials, USDA is not required to collect such data for these crops.

[b] We could not calculate the cost increases as a percentage of the production costs for these crops because of the missing data.

We note that the ultimate impact of such limited production cost increases on farmers' income would depend on their individual profit margins. However, for the industry as a whole, the impact on farmers' income appears to be minimal. For example, as noted in table 2, for a 5 to 20 percentage point reduction in subsidies, total farm costs in 2012 would have increased from about $0.4 billion to $1.8 billion.[23] Further, as discussed, farm sector income in 2012 was about $114 billion. Thus, these increased costs, as a percentage of farm sector income, would have been about 0.4 to 1.6 percent.

Impact to Farmers' Participation in the Crop Insurance Program Resulting from Premium Subsidy Reductions May Be Minimal

Information on the impact to farmer participation from reductions in federal crop insurance premium subsidies is limited, but the economic literature and government information that is available suggest the impact may be minimal. Farm industry groups and some researchers have stated that changes to crop insurance premium subsidies could result in reductions in farmer participation and insurance coverage levels. However, available economic literature on the impact on farmer participation due to premium subsidy reductions indicates that farmers' response to changes in premium subsidies may be small due to factors such as their heavy reliance on crop insurance, the attractiveness of revenue policies, and the increasing importance of crop insurance as other farm programs are reduced or eliminated.

Government studies of this issue have reached similar conclusions. A limited RMA analysis in support of the president's 2014 budget proposal determined that a 5 percentage point premium subsidy reduction for yield and revenue policies would result in a limited number of farmers leaving the crop insurance program; that analysis determined that it was more likely that some farmers would purchase lower levels of policy coverage. According to RMA's Chief Actuary, it is difficult to determine the effect of a premium subsidy change in part because of the lack of data. The task of determining the effect of a change is easier if there has been a major change in premium subsidy rates, and the impact can be assessed, this official said. A major change in premium subsidy rates creates a "natural experiment" in which to better analyze the impact to farmer participation from a change in subsidy rates. According to the Chief Actuary, this "natural experiment" last occurred with the passage of the Agricultural Risk Protection Act in 2000 that significantly raised premium subsidy rates. This in turn led to an increase in farmer participation in the crop insurance program. However, there has been no "natural experiment" to analyze how reduced premium subsidy rates impact farmer participation because, since 2000, premium subsidy rates generally have not been reduced.[24] In the event that premium subsidy rates were reduced, actual information on the impact on farmer participation would be available. According to an RMA official, it would be a good idea to monitor the impact on farmer participation if Congress reduced premium subsidy rates.

CBO, in its 2013 report on options for reducing the federal deficit, also determined that cutting premium subsidies for crop insurance policies would not have a substantial effect on farmer participation in the program.[25] Furthermore, a 2013 independent study by an ERS economist of the impact on farmer participation of reductions in premium subsidies noted that the overall demand for crop insurance appeared to be relatively unaffected by moderately small changes in premium subsidies.[26] In addition, this study estimated that if there was a 5 percent reduction in crop insurance premium subsidies, corn farmers would drop insurance coverage for about 3 percent of their acres (i.e., leave the crop insurance program), soybean farmers would drop coverage for about 2 percent of their acres, and wheat farmers would drop coverage for about 4 percent of their acres.[27] However, the study further noted that, because farmers rely heavily on crop insurance, these results could overestimate the potential impact to farmer participation and the overall number of farmers leaving the crop insurance program could be smaller.

Stakeholder and government officials we interviewed, as well as documents and data we reviewed, have identified several different incentives that could lessen the likelihood of significant changes in farmer participation in the crop insurance program even if premium subsidies are reduced. First, even with the premium subsidy reduction, farmers would receive substantial premium subsidies for revenue policies. For example, with a premium subsidy reduction of 20 percentage points for revenue policies, farmers would receive an average premium subsidy rate of about 40 percent for their premium cost, based on our analysis of 2012 RMA data. Second, crop insurance is important to lenders that provide loans to farmers to help finance their operations. According to lending associations that represent agriculture credit providers, crop insurance provides lenders with greater certainty that loans made to farmers will be repaid. In addition, according to an economic paper published by two ERS economists and a professor from the University of Illinois, [28] participation in crop insurance lowers revenue risk and might allow lenders to accept loan applications with lower collateral or applications for farm operations that are more leveraged. Third, farmers may not be inclined to exit the crop insurance program since it has emerged as the main safety net for farmers. According to some farm industry stakeholders, many farmers have made crop insurance their primary risk management tool. Finally, another incentive for farmer participation may be growing concerns among farmers about the frequency and severity of adverse weather events, such as floods, droughts, heat waves, and strong storms. According to the Secretary of Agriculture, other USDA officials, and some state extension officials and academic researchers, farmers are increasingly concerned about such weather events and their impact on agricultural production, including crop losses.

CONCLUSION

Federal crop insurance plays an important role in protecting farmers from losses caused by natural disasters and price declines, and it has become one of the most important programs in the farm safety net for farmers, according to USDA officials and some farm industry stakeholders. However, with increasing budgetary pressures, it is critical that federal resources are targeted as effectively as possible. With record farm income in recent years, the subsidies, including premium subsidies, provided for federal crop insurance have come under increasing scrutiny. Reductions in premium subsidies for farmers who purchase revenue policies, the most common and expensive crop insurance policy type, present an opportunity to potentially save hundreds of millions of dollars per year for taxpayers with limited increases in individual farmer's production costs. The president has included proposals for premium subsidy reductions in his fiscal year 2013, 2014, and 2015 budgets. Such a change would require congressional action and could either be implemented immediately, as in 2000, when Congress enacted legislation to increase premium subsidy rates, or phased in, as when RMA increases the premiums charged for crop insurance policies based on new actuarial data.

One point of discussion in the debate over premium subsidy reductions is the possible impact on farmer participation in the program. The crop insurance industry and some researchers suggest that even a modest premium subsidy reduction would result in some farmers lowering their coverage levels or dropping coverage altogether. However, the administration, CBO, and other researchers say that a modest reduction in premium subsidies would have little impact on program participation, and that incentives, such as the continued high level of premium subsidies, would likely keep farmers in the program. Although the impact of such a reduction is unknown, in the event that Congress reduced the crop insurance premium subsidy rates, actual information on the impact on farmer participation would be available if participation were monitored.

MATTER FOR CONGRESSIONAL CONSIDERATION

To reduce the cost of the crop insurance program and achieve budgetary savings for deficit reduction or other purposes, Congress should consider reducing the level of federal premium subsidies for revenue crop insurance policies. In doing so, Congress should consider whether to make the full amount of this reduction in an initial year, or to phase in the full amount of this reduction over several years. In addition, Congress should consider directing the Secretary of Agriculture to monitor and report on the impact, if any, of the reduction on farmer participation in the crop insurance program.

AGENCY COMMENTS AND OUR EVALUATION

We provided the Secretary of Agriculture with a draft of this report for review and comment. In its written comments, USDA said it had no comment with the report's findings. In addition, USDA provided technical comments, which we incorporated as appropriate.

Sincerely yours,
Anne-Marie Fennell
Director, Natural Resources and Environment

APPENDIX I: OBJECTIVES, SCOPE, AND METHODOLOGY

Our objectives were to examine (1) trends in federal crop insurance costs and farm sector income and wealth from 2003 through 2012 and (2) the potential savings to the government and impacts to farmers, if any, of reducing federal premium subsidies for revenue insurance policies.

To address these objectives, we interviewed officials of the U.S. Department of Agriculture (USDA), including officials from the Economic Research Service (ERS) and Risk Management Agency (RMA), and reviewed documents they provided such as, for example, crop insurance program costs and outlays documents. We also spoke with officials at the Congressional Budget Office (CBO).

To address our first objective, we reviewed and analyzed RMA data on the government's cost for the federal crop insurance program for the period 2003 through 2012. We are reporting federal crop insurance program costs, not outlays, because the cost numbers more accurately reflect the true costs for a given year. For example, much of the actual costs for 2012 were not determined until the following year after the claims adjustments were completed and the underwriting gains and losses determined. In contrast, outlays for 2012 do not include many of the costs actually incurred that year, but they do include many costs incurred the prior year (i.e., 2011) because of the lag time in completing the claims adjustments for that year. Finally, in reporting costs, not outlays, we are being consistent with how the program reports its costs, including in the audited financial statements of the Federal Crop Insurance Corporation. We analyzed RMA crop insurance program data including data on the level of premium subsidies for revenue policies, the top

10 states that received revenue policy premium subsidies, the insurance coverage levels chosen by farmers with revenue policies, and the crops that received the most revenue policy premium subsidies. For overall program costs, we analyzed fiscal year data presented in RMA's cost and outlay tables. RMA data contain more detailed crop insurance information by crop year, which is what we used for our revenue policy analyses. For these analyses, we only included information on "buy-up" policies—that is, the portion of crop insurance for which a farmer pays a premium. Any coverage that is purchased above the "catastrophic" level is considered "buy-up" coverage; this type of coverage represented 99.9 percent of the revenue policy premium subsidies for the 2003 through 2012 period. In addition, we only included information for individual revenue policies and excluded group revenue policies because these latter policies made up only a small portion (less than 2 percent) of the total premium subsidies associated with revenue policies. We selected the time period of 2003 through 2012 to get a representation of the trend in program costs, usage of revenue policies, and financial condition of the farm sector. At the time of our analysis, USDA officials said that 2012 would be the most recent year with complete and stable crop insurance program data. To get an understanding of trends in farm sector income and wealth, we reviewed and analyzed ERS data and reports on the overall financial condition of the farm sector, including information on net farm and cash income, production costs, and farm debt ratios from 2003 through 2012, as well as information from USDA's National Agricultural Statistics Service on farmland values for these years. We also reviewed and analyzed ERS information on forecasts for these elements of the farm economy, including net cash income and net farm income for 2013 and 2014. For the purposes of this report, crop insurance costs and premium subsidies, which are budget-related data, are reported in nominal dollars, while data on median farm household and U.S. household income, net farm and net cash income, and farmland values are reported in inflation adjusted dollars, using 2012 as the reference year. In addition, as appropriate, we report these data in calendar, fiscal, or crop years,[1] depending on how the data were reported in the source documents. Unless otherwise indicated, these data are in calendar years.

To address our second objective, we analyzed RMA revenue policy crop insurance program data for 2012 to estimate the savings to the federal government from reductions in premium subsidies of 5, 10, 15, and 20 percentage points. We selected these percentages because they were in line with previous reductions proposed by the president's 2014 budget proposal, a 2013 CBO report,[2] and a 2012 GAO report.[3] We also estimated the additional production cost per acre, on average, and by crop type, to individual farmers as a result of these premium subsidy reductions. Furthermore, we compared these additional production costs with the total cost of production, on average, and by crop, to determine the percentage increase represented by these additional production costs. We used ERS Agricultural Resource Management Survey data for 2012, where available, to determine the average production costs, per acre, for barley, canola, corn, cotton, grain sorghum, popcorn, rice, soybeans, sunflowers, and wheat. These were the crops eligible to receive revenue policy premium subsidies during the period covered by our review. We also reviewed the available agricultural economic literature,[4] and studies by CBO, ERS, and RMA, and we spoke with officials from those agencies to determine any potential savings from reductions in crop insurance premium subsidies and the impact, if any, on farmers' participation in the crop insurance program as a result of premium subsidy reductions. Finally, we reviewed documents from farm industry stakeholders on the crop insurance program.

For the various data used in our analyses, as discussed, we generally reviewed related documentation, interviewed knowledgeable officials, and reviewed related internal controls information to evaluate the reliability of these data. In each case, we concluded that the data were sufficiently reliable for the purposes of this report.

We conducted this performance audit from May 2013 to August 2014 in accordance with generally accepted government auditing standards. Those standards require that we plan and perform the audit to obtain sufficient, appropriate evidence to provide a reasonable basis for our findings and conclusions based on our audit objectives. We believe that the evidence obtained provides a reasonable basis for our findings and conclusions based on our objectives.

End Notes

[1] According to the Department of the Treasury's Bureau of the Fiscal Service, as of March 2014, the total national debt was estimated at $17.6 trillion, including $12.6 trillion in debt held by the public. These mid-fiscal year amounts have not been audited.

[2] See http://www.gao.gov/fiscal_outlook/overview.

[3] GAO, 2013 Annual Report: Actions Needed to Reduce Fragmentation, Overlap, and Duplication and Achieve Other Financial Benefits, GAO-13-279SP (Washington, D.C.: Apr. 9, 2013); Crop Insurance: Savings Would Result from Program Changes and Greater Use of Data Mining, GAO-12-256 (Washington, D.C.: Mar. 13, 2012).

[4] We used USDA data for the period 2003 through 2012 to get a representation of the trend in program costs, usage of revenue policies, and financial condition of the farm sector. At the

time of our review, 2012 was the most recent year with complete and stable crop insurance data, according to RMA officials

[5] The most basic level of coverage is "catastrophic" coverage; premiums for these policies are completely subsidized by the federal government. Under "catastrophic" policies, the farmer receives a payment for losses greater than 50 percent of "normal" yield indemnified at 55 percent of the estimated market price of the crop. Farmers can select to "buy-up" higher levels of insurance coverage for protection against wider yield or revenue losses; they pay a premium for these "buy-up" policies.

[6] According to ERS, a crop year (also known as a marketing year) is the 12-month period starting with the month when the harvest of a specific crop typically begins. For example, the 2008 wheat crop year was June 1, 2008 through May 30, 2009.

[7] We reviewed the agricultural economic literature for the period 1993 through 2013 because the studies within this time frame have more relevance to the current crop insurance program.

[8] RMA defines crop insurance penetration as a comparison of insured acres to planted acres.

[9] Farmers select a coverage level—that is, the percentage of their normal yield or revenue they want to insure. In 2012, more than half of the enrolled corn and soybean acres were at coverage levels above 70 percent.

[10] R. Dismukes and J. Glauber, "Why Hasn't Crop Insurance Eliminated Disaster Assistance?", Amber Waves, USDA Economic Research Service (June 2005).

[11] Generally, individual crop insurance coverage is available at levels ranging from 50 to 85 percent, at 5 percent increments, e.g., 50 percent, 55 percent, 60 percent, etc.

[12] According to RMA officials, the Federal Crop Insurance Act provides guidelines on the types of crops that are eligible for federal crop insurance.

[13] USDA's Federal Crop Insurance Corporation Board of Directors approved the Pulse Crop Revenue Endorsements on March 1, 2012, providing revenue policy coverage for dry beans and dry peas starting in crop year 2013.

[14] A median amount means half the households had incomes that were higher, and half had incomes that were lower than that figure.

[15] Net cash income is forecast to decline less than net farm income primarily because net cash income reflects the sale of more than $6 billion in carryover stocks from 2013. Net farm income reflects only the earnings from production that occurred in the current year.

[16] For a description of the Corn Belt region, see map in figure 6.

[17] Production costs include, among other things, the cost of fertilizer, pesticides, fuel, labor, seed, and insurance.

[18] On a policy-by-policy basis, the new rates took effect as individual farmer policies came up for renewal, according to RMA officials.

[19] According to RMA documents, as a result of a premium rate study that was completed in 2011, RMA made adjustments to the premium rates of several crops including corn, soybeans, and wheat. RMA was concerned about the effect on the program if the changes were too dramatic and decided to phase in the rate adjustments.

[20] GAO-12-256.

[21] Specifically, the second proposal applied to revenue policies that include the harvest price provision. Such policies accounted for about 98 percent of the premium subsidies for all revenue policies in 2012.

[22] CBO, Options for Reducing the Deficit: 2014 to 2023 (Washington, D.C.: November 2013).

[23] Table 2 amounts that show the potential savings to the government from premium subsidy rate reductions also represent the increase in total farm costs as a result of those reductions.

[24] According to RMA officials, the subsidy rate for the risk income group policy was reduced in 2008 and then again in 2009. For example, in 2008, the rate was reduced by 5 percentage points for the 75 percent coverage level. This type of policy makes up a relatively small component of the crop insurance program; in 2008, acres insured with this group policy accounted for 2.4 percent of the total insured acres. The reduction of the subsidy rate corresponded with a decrease in the number of acres insured with this type of policy, according to RMA officials. This may have been especially true after 2008 when the subsidy rate was increased for enterprise unit individual coverage, such as an 80 percent subsidy rate for a 70 percent coverage level.

[25] CBO, Options for Reducing the Deficit: 2014 to 2023 (Washington, D.C.: November 2013).

[26] Erik J. O'Donoghue, The Demand for Crop Insurance: How Important are the Subsidies? Selected paper prepared for presentation at the Agricultural & Applied Economics Association's 2013 Crop Insurance and the Farm Bill Symposium (Louisville, KY: Oct. 8-9, 2013).

[27] ERS published a study in July 2014 that reached similar conclusions. This study generally showed a lower effect on farmer participation in the crop insurance program as a result of a 5 percent reduction in premium subsidies than shown in the 2013 independent study. See ERS, The Effects of Premium Subsidies on Demand for Crop Insurance, Economic Research Report 169 (Washington, D.C.: July 2014).

[28] Jennifer Ifft, Todd Kuethe, and Mitch Morehart, Farm Debt Use by Farms with Crop Insurance. Choices, Agricultural & Applied Economics Association (3rd Quarter 2013).

End Notes for Appendix I

[1] According to ERS, a crop year (also known as a marketing year) is the 12-month period starting with the month when the harvest of a specific crop typically begins. For example, the 2008 wheat crop year was June 1, 2008 through May 30, 2009.

[2] CBO, Options for Reducing the Deficit: 2014 to 2023 (Washington, D.C.: November 2013).

[3] GAO, Crop Insurance: Savings Would Result from Program Changes and Greater Use of Data Mining, GAO-12-256 (Washington, D.C.: Mar. 13, 2012).

[4] As the focus of our work was on the sensitivity of farmer participation in the crop insurance program to changes in premium subsidies, we selected studies relevant to that question. The studies we reviewed were published between 1993 and 2013— approximately the past 20 years. The literature goes back further, but the more recent studies have more relevance to the current crop insurance program. In order to ensure the studies were reliable and reputable, we considered mainly studies that were published in peer-reviewed publications or by federal agencies. In addition, the studies were reviewed by GAO's Chief Economist, who is an expert in the area of agricultural economics, and another GAO senior economist.

INDEX

S

T

U

V

W

Y